Building a Fireplace

Step-by-Step Instructions for Contemporary to Classic Styles

Bernd Grützmacher

4880 Lower Valley Road, Atglen, PA 19310 USA

Library of Congress Cataloging-in-Publication Data

Grützmacher, Bernd.
  Building a fireplace : step-by-step instructions for
contemporary to classic styles / by Bernd Grutzmacher.
      p. cm.
  ISBN 0-7643-2081-5 (pbk.)
  1. Fireplaces—Design and construction. I. Title.
TH7425.G78 2004
749'.62—dc22

2004009804

Originally published by Georg D.W. Callwey GmbH & Co.
KG, Streitfeldstrasse 35, 81673 Munich, Germany.

Translated by Dr. Edward Force, Central Connecticut State
University

Designed by Mark David Bowyer
Type set in Humanist521 BT / Aldine721 BT

ISBN: 0-7643-2081-5
Printed in China

Published by Schiffer Publishing Ltd.
4880 Lower Valley Road
Atglen, PA 19310
Phone: (610) 593-1777; Fax: (610) 593-2002
E-mail: Info@schifferbooks.com

For the largest selection of fine reference books on this and
related subjects, please visit our web site at
www.schifferbooks.com
We are always looking for people to write books on new and
related subjects. If you have an idea for a book please contact
us at the above address.

This book may be purchased from the publisher.
Include $3.95 for shipping.
Please try your bookstore first.
You may write for a free catalog.

In Europe, Schiffer books are distributed by
Bushwood Books
6 Marksbury Ave.
Kew Gardens
Surrey TW9 4JF England
Phone: 44 (0) 20 8392-8585; Fax: 44 (0) 20 8392-9876
E-mail: info@bushwoodbooks.co.uk
Free postage in the U.K., Europe; air mail at cost.

Contents

Foreword

A flickering fire in the fireplace is an experience for the senses – a relaxing source of heat that invites conversation and brings forth pleasant memories – a fireplace fire is pure atmosphere!

Whoever would like to realize the primal experience of a fire in an old or a new home will find ideas and encouragement in this book to ease the fireplace planning process, including talks with a fireplace builder. Planning and building a fireplace should be entrusted only to a master of the tile oven building trade, who will realize individual concepts in cooperation with local building codes.

Fireplaces reflect every homeowner's unique and individual style. Throughout this book, the author documents a variety of different fireplace styles. In the first part of the book, readers will enjoy projects that show the construction of "open" fireplaces in the traditional manner – from the country-house style to an Italian design.

In the second part of the book, "Flames Behind Glass," the author illustrates the construction of wood stoves, in which the fire crackles and flames behind glass, efficiently utilizing wooden bundles of energy to heat a room. This section includes a fireplace visible from two rooms, an ideal design for families with small children.

In the last part, "Open Fireplaces in Free Style," the construction of two "heat sculptures" is documented, featuring examples of handmade constructions borrowed from the "ground oven of heavy structure."

The first example, "Warm Sculpture in White," is particularly interesting: The room-high open fireplace was built and finished from a 1:10-scale model. The second example is a combination of heat conserving oven and open fireplace, whose simple rustic design will interest those who have building talent and want to reduce building costs by doing the job themselves.

Open Fireplaces

in Traditional Style

Fireplace 1:

A Wedding Present for the Bride and Groom

After the master builder inherited the stonecutting yard from his father and began specializing in the constuction of energy efficient houses, his wife's longtime wish could be fulfilled: a traditional open fireplace with an Italian façade cut from the finest marble – finely polished and perfectly installed by a master. This was the wedding present from the retired master stonecutter.

Fig. 1: The finished fireplace in the living room.

Surface, Structure, and Detail Drawings

Even though the classic open fireplace is seldom built anymore (either because the heat production is very meager or because the fire requires constant care), the building of an open fireplace is documented here to make the traditional building method clear. After determining the fireplace's functional and stylistic details, which in this case include the Italian fireplace façade (Pompeii model), the master builder can begin the job once the following drawings and sketches are available:

1. Baseplate
2. Lower inner frame member
3, 4. Side frame members
5, 6. Uprights of the fireplace façade
7. Upper frame member
8. Mantelpiece

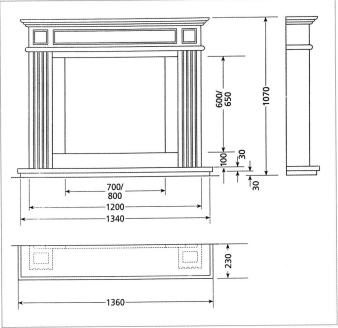

Fig. 2: Fireplace façade style, from three sides.

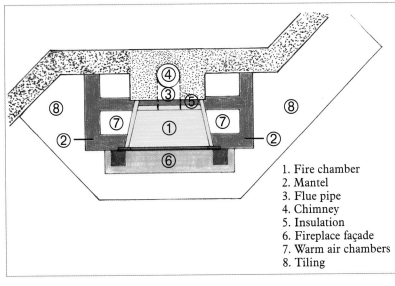

Fig. 3: Individual parts of the fireplace façade.

Fig. 4: Master builder's ground plan (construction drawing).

1. Fire chamber
2. Mantel
3. Flue pipe
4. Chimney
5. Insulation
6. Fireplace façade
7. Warm air chambers
8. Tiling

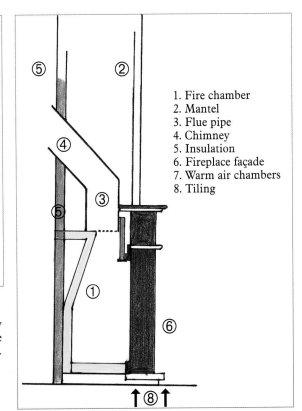

Fig. 5: Cutaway drawing: façade, fire chamber, and flue.

1. Fire chamber
2. Mantel
3. Flue pipe
4. Chimney
5. Insulation
6. Fireplace façade
7. Warm air chambers
8. Tiling

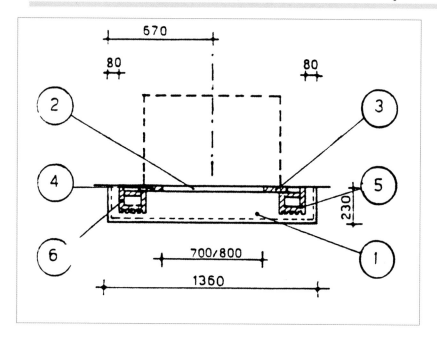

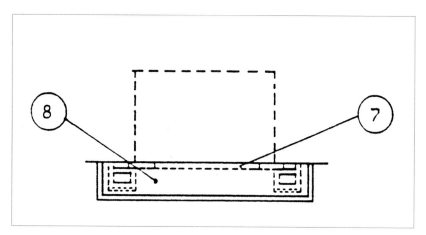

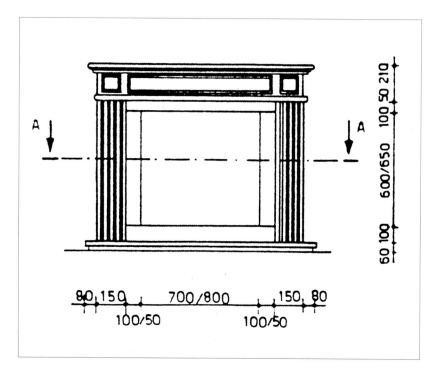

Guide to Building

and Making it Real

In the Italian manufacturer's building instructions, the following sequence is recommended for assembling the fireplace façade, provided that the baseplate is made of masonry, and that it is clearly marked with the fire chamber lines.

—Set the double baseplate (1) in mortar at the rim of the fire chamber.
—Set the lower interior frame member (2) high on the baseplate.
—Set the pillars (5 and 6) up vertically and attach to the fire chamber walls. (Author's note: the extension joint is missing!)
—Fit the inner frame members (3, 4, 7) in horizontally and vertically with marble cement.
—Attach the mantelpiece (8).

Important tip: The fireplace façade and fire chamber must be separated by an extension joint, which is filled out with a ceramic thickening band.

The Italian manufacturer's detailed drawings, Fig. 6a, 6b, and 6c, are spread out to make this series of operations visible, whereby it should be noted that the sequence is somewhat closer together in reality. Such drawings offer important information to the stove and fireplace builder. Only through these are exact drawings possible (see Fig. 4 and 5), in which the constructive details and masses are included. But now to the actual practice.

Fig. 6a-c: Instructions for assembling the fireplace façade.

Building the
Base and Fire Chamber

Building the Base

In the first step of the work, the ground dimensions of the fireplace are marked on the part of the concrete floor that is not occupied by insulation plates and concrete for this project. The fireplace builder built the masonry base on which the marble baseplate (1) was laid in lime mortar with lime-sandstone (Format: 2DF).

It was important here that the lower edge of the marble baseplate (1) had the same height as the future parquet.

As soon as the 2.6-in. (60 mm) thick baseplate was laid horizontally in lime mortar, which set quickly, the lower inside frame member (2) was provisionally set vertically on the baseplate (height 4 in. or 100 mm), so as to be able to determine the exact height of the fire chamber base. As Fig. 10 shows, some 4 in. (10.5cm to 11.0 cm) remained for building up the fire chamber base.

In the center of the picture, the 2.5-in. (6 cm) thick baseplate can be seen with the lower frame member's top edge (height: 4 in. or 10 cm); to the right are the 1.5-in. (4 cm) thick lightweight concrete plates (Ytong), which were set in thin-layer mortar.

Before construction of the fire chamber base began, the laid marble plate had to be protected and the Ytong situation covered with aluminum foil, so as to reflect future heat radiation or block its way downward. Instead of aluminum foil, ceramic fiber felt is used more and more today.

Fig. 7: Building the base of the open fireplace. In the foreground is the buildup for the baseplate, in the background is the chimney structure.

Fig. 8: Lime mortar bed for the baseplate, which can be seen in the background.

Fig. 9: Hand-locating the baseplate (positioning the lower edge at the same level as the upper edge of the parquet). In the foreground, the level stands on part of the parquet (with temporary joint reinforcement).

Fig. 10: Provisional setting up of the lower parts of the frame, to determine the dimensions of the fire chamber.

Fig. 11: Laying out the heat-reflecting aluminum foil; in the foreground is the shielded marble plate.

This builder began to work on this reflecting situation with the building of the fire chamber base by laying soft burned clay tiles of plaster mortar – instead of heavy plaster tiles – *flat*, in order to prepare the final height of the fire chamber base exactly.

Fig. 12: Laying the bricks in fire-clay mortar on the aluminum foil.

Fig. 13: In front is the shielded marble plate; in back are the bricks.

Beginning to Build the Fire Chamber

The first step of the work consisted of marking the fire chamber outline on the brick layer to be able to set the base of the fire chamber walls in fireplace mortar. For this, 1-in. (2.5 cm) thick fire-clay plates were used (see Fig. 14 and 15).

In Fig. 15, the completed base for the fire chamber and its opening can be seen: in the foreground is the shielded marble plate on the sandstone, in the background is the brick layer with the baseplates.

Setting the

Fire Chamber Walls

Before the fire chamber walls are set, it is advisable to loosely set the 1.6-in. (4 cm) thick slot and spring plates in order to determine the free gaps to the sixteenth of an inch and cut the matching plate parts exactly. At the same time, one should note how the fire-clay plates are to be set raised in the laid adhesive. After these preliminaries, the first layer of the fire chamber wall can be set vertically in fireplace mortar (see Fig. 16 and 17).

In Fig. 18, not only the rear wall set in the adhesive, but also the beginning of the lateral (hot-air) uprights can be seen, which directly adjoin the fire chamber wall. In the background the not-yet insulated chimney block can be seen.

Fig. 14: Laying the baseplates for the fire chamber walls.

Fig. 15: Horizontal baseplates for the fire chamber walls.

Fig. 16: Loosely positioned fire chamber plates, in order to determine the fit.

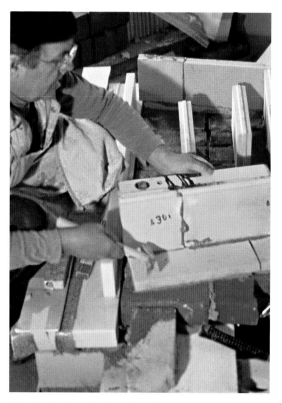

Fig. 17: Setting the first fire chamber plates.

The first step of building the fire chamber in Fig. 19 is even clearer, as the construction of the side columns can be seen. It is interesting that the two-sided columns were set in cement mortar, but the contact with the fire chamber wall was made with heat resistant fast-setting mortar in order to avoid cracks from bending and to guarantee the stability of the fire chamber wall. Up to this point, the trapezoid-shaped fire chamber wall had a height of 12 in. (30 cm). From that height up, the rear fire chamber wall was supposed to be set with a slight inclination to the front (about 75 instead of 90 degrees). Thus the fireplace builder cut thin wedges that he set on the chimney block with quick-setting mortar before the fire-clay plates measuring 12.6 in. x 6 in. x 1.6 in. (32cm x 15cm x 4 cm) could be set. In Fig. 20 this process is shown, and we can conclude that the builder has marked the 11.8-in. (30 cm) height line as the first "folding line." It is also important that these fire-clay plates were laid horizontally.

Fig. 18: The fire chamber wall after the first step, with the second (still) vertical back wall in the rear.

Fig. 19: The fireplace construction after the second step.

Fig. 20: Beginning of the back wall of the fire chamber, which tilts forward. The insulating and reflecting shield is between the wedges.

Fig. 21: The fire chamber after the third step.

In order to carry out the following step to the sixteenth of an inch, the master builder used one of his drawings in 1:10 scale. In order to determine the heights, angles, and distances exactly; they were marked in 1:1 scale on a board.

The second "folding line" was then the upper edge of the third row, in order to attain a final tilt of the fire chamber's rear wall of about 70 degrees with the fourth row (see Fig. 24).

In order to stabilize this tilted construction to the chimney block, the builder used cut bricks that were set in fire-clay mortar, although quick-setting mortar would have been especially suited for this.

Fig. 22: Taking the dimensions from the drawings for the further construction.

Fig. 24: The fourth row of the fire chamber's back wall, set at a 70-degree angle; the hot air columns are to the left and right. In the center are the support and "help board" (see Fig. 23).

Fig. 23: Height and tilt angle for the first construction are marked on a vertical board.

Fig. 25: An angle-stabilizing wedge for the tilted back wall of the fire chamber.

Fig. 26: Setting the fifth row (back wall of the fire chamber).★
Above: The chimney connection, diameter 9.8 in. (25 cm).

★Note: For the back wall of the fire chamber, a rule of thumb is to "pull it" 1/3 of the height vertically and 2/3 to the front, setting it at an angle. It is astonishing that this tip is not mentioned in the instructions for building open fireplaces!

After the rear and side walls of the fire chamber – including the fifth row – were set at a height of about 25.6 in. (65 cm), the builder finished the two lateral hot-air columns in order to then concentrate on the marble façade of the open fireplace.

Setting the Fireplace Façade

So as not to confuse the reader with the façade builder's building instructions, the everyday practice will be noted here: In this example, the fireplace builder set the fire chamber walls and the side enclosures, which simultaneously will be hot air columns, at a level that is necessary to complete the fireplace façade.

In Fig. 27, the situation *before* these steps is shown.

In Fig. 28, it can be seen that the columns (6) were set vertically on the baseplate (1) against the lower inside frames (2). While the marble pieces were linked to each other with a marble adhesive, the builder used quick-setting mortar and ceramic fiber strips to link the marble columns to the fire chamber walls. This left the vertical inside frame member (4) with a sufficient joint, which was provided by the lower frame member. The same process was repeated on the right side of the fireplace before the fire chamber was completed and the façade could be finished.

Fig. 27: The fireplace construction before setting the fine marble façade.

Fig. 28: Vertical setting of the left marble upright.

Fig. 29: Vertical setting of the left inner frame.

Fig. 30: With quick-setting mortar, the builder links the marble columns (and inner frame) with the fire chamber walls.

Fig. 31: The connection between the marble column (left) and the adjoining fire chamber wall in the center, with the chimney block at right.

Fig. 32: The fireplace after setting the columns (5,6) and lateral inside frames (3,4).

Fig. 33: The upper frame member (left) and the finished back wall of the fire chamber (right center). The heat-reflecting insulation layer is on the chimney side.

Fig. 35: Vertically checking the horizontal mantelpiece.

Fig. 36: Cleaning the joint between the upper interior space and the mantelpiece.

After the two marble columns and lateral inside frames were stabilized vertically at equal heights, the upper frame member (7) and then the mantel could be set horizontally.

To stabilize the upper frame member quickly in its horizontal and vertical position, it was set in marble mortar on both columns (Fig. 33).

In Fig. 34, the final form of the fireplace becomes visible. To finish it, the last part of the back wall was set with a complete, reinforced fire-clay plate, which can be seen in Fig. 33 to the right of the upper fireplace frame, and in Fig. 34 right behind the upper frame. And since this last part of the rear wall was only 0.8 in. (2 cm) thick, the builder later filled in the rear area with two fire-clay plates laid together (0.6 in. or 15 mm thick), to maintain the previous thickness of 1.6 in. (4 cm).

Fig. 34: The fireplace after the upper inside frame was set.

Fig. 37: The temporarily installed flue pipe, with the shielded fireplace façade in the foreground.

The Hood and

Chimney Connection

Preparatory work was necessary before the fireplace hood, where the smoke of the fire would be conducted into the chimney, could be finished. This included reinforcing the last row of the fire chamber's tilted back wall, its horizontal covering to the chimney, and the sub-construction for the flue pipe, 9.8 in. (25 cm) in diameter, still to be installed.

Note that the flue pipe was attached to the chimney connection with quick-setting mortar. Fig. 38 illustrates how the builder formed the vertical bottom plate of fireplace mortar to aid the flow.

One special detail should be noted before the hood is built. To protect the back of the upper fireplace façade (inside frame

Fig. 38: The mount for the flue pipe is set with fireplace mortar and fire-clay plates.

Fig. 39: Details below the flue pipe, from right to left: The shielded marble mantel, the aluminum foil, reinforced fire-clay plate, and to the left the 5.5 in. (14 cm) wide and 25.2 in./31.5-in. (64/80 cm) long trapezoidal fire chamber opening.

Fig. 40: Building the fireplace hood of double-sided fire-clay plates. At upper left is the lever for the choke flap at the bend in the flue pipe.

Fig. 41: Fireplace and hood construction after the chimney connection.

Fig. 42: Sealing and smoothing the joints inside the fireplace hood.

and mantel) from the future heat, the builder set a completely reinforced fire-clay plate. Between this protective (strike) plate and the upper marble parts, he also put an insulation plate wrapped in heat-reflecting aluminum foil (see Fig. 39 right). The trapezoidal fireplace hood, also known as the smoke collector, was laid in a two-layered fire-clay plate construction (first layer: 1.6 in. or 4.0 cm, second layer: 1 in. or 2.5 cm) in fireplace mortar, as seen in Fig. 40 and 41.

Before joints and surfaces of the hood were finally made impervious to smoke and sealed, the builder decided to completely seal the inner joints of the hood and smooth them.

After that, the outer joints and adjoining surfaces of the hood could be sealed with fireplace mortar and smoothed.

Fig. 43: Sealing, grouting, and smoothing the outer fire chamber hood.

Fig. 44: Fiberglass armament fabric (grid size 0.4 in. x 0.4 in. or 10mm x 10 mm).

Fig. 45: Fire testing before installing the bottom of the fire chamber.

In order to avoid any heat-caused crack formation in the hood (since temperatures of 900 degress Farenheit or 500 degrees Celsius are common in this area), the builder decided to add armament fabric to the hood,

set in quick-setting mortar and finally covered with an extra layer of mortar.

Armament fabric and quick-setting mortar not only provide a heat-resistant covering for the hood, but also further the flowing speed of the future flames and smoke into the chimney. A test fire became the final step of this phase.

Fireplace Façade and Shape

Among the finishing tasks are the cutting and fitting of the fire-clay plates for the fire chamber floor, finishing the fireplace façade from the marble mantel up to the ceiling, installing a heat-insulating layer above the bend in the smoke pipe (Fig. 48), and plastering the marble-free surfaces with heat-resistant modeling plaster.

Fig. 47: The fire chamber floor made of fire-clay plates.

Fig. 46: The fireplace structure
while the fire chamber floor is laid.

Fig. 48: Above the bend in the flue pipe, the
master builder builds a heat-insulating layer.

Fig. 49: The fireplace covered with modeling
plaster before the artwork.

Fireplace 2:

The Corner Fireplace of a Farmhouse

Whoever builds his home in a wooded region near a merry brook can have not only central heating with wood but also an open fireplace that brings the "romance of hearth fire" into the living milieu.

Fig. 50: The country house after occupancy; at left is the chimney for the open fireplace. (Photo: Peter Hackenberg)

Fig. 51: The first fireplace fire after moving in. (Photo: Peter Hackenberg)

Chimney and
Fireplace Foundation

In the planning phase, the homeowner decided not only for cost-cutting do-it-yourself work, but also for a house with two chimneys, one for the central heating and the second for the open fireplace.

Because a large fireplace opening was wanted, the building inspector recommended an interior diameter of at least 13 ft. (4 m) from the smoke connection on, and a fresh-air pipe with a diameter of 7.9 in. (20 cm).

Oven installers and potters are usually ready if the architect or builder cannot decide at what height the smoke from the fireplace should be led into the chimney.

To avoid needless expenses, the author recommends consulting the fireplace builder and building inspector before the job is planned so as to define the final structure and the costs clearly.

Building a Base
for an Open Fireplace

After the final shape of the fireplace was cleared with the homeowner, the work began with the building of the base, for which four work processes were necessary.

In the first step, the potter constructed a base of perforated bricks as a foundation on the asphalt bottom layer. In the second step, the bricks were covered with so-called "Hourdis plates" (heat-resistant clay plates) (Fig. 54-56). In order to cut off the heat of the future fire toward the bottom, the surface was covered with ceramic felt. This was covered with fire-clay plates, 1.2 in. (3 cm) thick, set in fire chamber mortar. This extremely heat-resistant mortar was used because very high temperatures can affect the material in this layer.

Fig. 53: The homeowner and fireplace builders go over the last details of the future fireplace on the site.

Fig. 52: The separate chimney in the future fireplace room.

Fig. 54: Beginning to build the base with perforated bricks.

Fig. 55: The brick layout before the Hourdis plates are laid. The air intake pipe can be seen at the right.

Fig. 56: The first Hourdis plate is prepared for cutting.

Building the Fire Chamber

Since the base of the fire chamber, the sidewalls, and the back wall should be made of just one layer of fire-clay bricks, the builder began by laying the fire-clay bricks for the base of the fire chamber, fitting the front bricks to the rounded shape of the fireplace.

Parallel to building the fire chamber, the adjoining sidewalls were built of perforated bricks and a fire-clay wall was made be-tween the back wall of the fire chamber and the chimney to block future heat from the fire chamber.

In Fig. 62, two constructive details that concern the outer shape and combustion in the fire chamber are shown. In Fig. 61, it already becomes clear that the sidewalls of the fire chamber form a smooth arc, which becomes clearer in Fig. 62, a structural detail that will define the shape of this fireplace. Also, Fig. 62 shows how the future fresh-air pipe can be regulated for optimal

Fig. 57: The wall of plates covered with heat-reflecting ceramic felt.

Fig. 58: Laying the fire-clay plates in fireplace mortar.

Fig. 59: Beginning the fire chamber base
with fire-clay plates laid flat.

Fig. 60: The fire chamber structure with flat (base) and high-
angled fire-clay bricks (walls). The fresh air intake is at the right.

Fig. 61: The fireplace takes form with adjacent sidewalls, the heat-reflecting wall, and the fresh-air pipe. In the foreground is the "smoke hood" or "smoke collector."

Fig. 62: The finished fire chamber of the fireplace before the "smoke collector" is installed.

Fig. 63: The hood (smoke collector), handmade by a metal smith and set by the potter, with the smoke pipe to the chimney. Below the hood the fresh-air grid can be seen.

burning: At the upper right of the fireplace's back wall, a fire-resistant cast iron grid can be seen, with which the combustion air is regulated manually. Some may question why the fresh air intake was installed adjacent to the smoke pipe rather than at a lower level in the fire chamber. This will be answered in further examples.

Now the builder continued his work by setting the hood (smoke collector), welded to size by a master metalworker, on the fire chamber walls. He had already applied fire-resistant ceramic felt to them. The material is not only flexible, but also seals the joint between the fire chamber wall and the hood.

Fig. 64: The builder adjusts the final position of the hood before it is installed with fire-resistant materials.

Fig. 65: The scene before the final covering; at left, the control rod for the choke flap is being cut.

Fig. 67: After the second mantel plate is laid, the potter completes the fireplace covering with fire-clay strips set at angles.

Fig. 66: Laying ceramic felt and quick-setting mortar on the first mantel plate prepares for the second plate, which is attached with quick-setting mortar. The fire-impervious ceramic caulking material lies between the mantel (ceramic) and hood (steel).

Fireplace Façade

Shape and Design

After the sheet-steel fireplace hood was installed and the curved flue pipe (diameter 9.8 in. or 25 cm) with the choke flap was attached to the chimney and sealed with quick-setting mortar, the builders began to build up the outer shape of the chimney to the upper edge of the hood and cover it with fire-clay plates. This surface was then to be the foundation of the chimney façade.

Fig. 68: The un-plastered fireplace covering of the semicircular corner fireplace before being covered with fire-clay plates.

Fig. 69: The lower part of the fireplace covered
with a reinforced fire-clay plate is already usable.

Fig. 70: Beginning to cover the
chimney with lightweight plates.

Before the covering was fitted, the mantel had to be cut to fit from large fire-clay plates and set in quick-setting mortar, in a double layer to continue the visual width of the sidewalls of the fire chamber, and also to make the mantel stronger.

The illustrations show the most important steps in the work.

After the rough construction of the fireplace was finished (Fig. 71) and the lime plaster could be applied by hand, the builder wanted to make the upper part of the fireplace a slimmer, rounded column, as the existing shape seemed too dominant to him. Designing and building the upper part were the result, and it is to be noted that the final form lost weightiness and gained elegance.

Fig. 71: The complete masonry of the chimney before the lime plastering. Here the final cleanup is being done.

Fig. 72: The first fire, after the plasterwork was applied by hand.
(Photo: Peter Hackenberg)

Fireplace 3:

An "English" Fireplace in an Older House

In a century-old structure with a double-walled brick exterior and circulating air layer, a roof of the finest carpentry work, and parquet floors of seasoned oak, the style of the open fireplace is merely a matter of Hanseatic understatement: Very British! But with an Italian marble façade.

Fig. 74: The fireplace on the builder's last workday.

Fig. 73: The open fireplace after the installation of the bookcases on the sides.

Drawings and Reality

In the Brennpunkt firm of Hamburg-Braak it is customary to plan, or "describe," every tile oven or fireplace project in detail before the work begins in order to carry out the work as disturbance-free as possible. This work description, which every fireplace builder receives before the work begins, includes not only scale drawings (see Fig. 75, front view, and Fig. 76, top view), but also precise directions for building the fireplace.

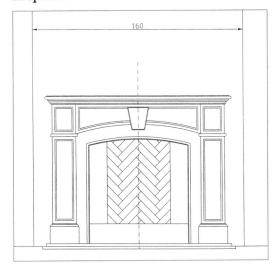

Fig. 75: Front view of the "English" fireplace with Italian-style façade.

Under the title of "Layout Description," the fireplace documented here is described as follows:

—Open fireplace with wall opening and styled façade, built of fire-bricks in herringbone pattern.

—Foundation must be built. Parquet was already removed.

—Connecting work (chimney connection): Connect the smoke passage with 9.8-in. (250 mm) pipe to *the two chimneys*!

—Air intake work: install in the foundation to the side within the air layer of the masonry (with fresh air grid in the outside wall).

Under the heading of "Otherwise/Special Features," constructive details are defined: How the height of the fireplace apron (above the fire chamber) is to be built so that it is even with the upper edge of the window opening. The combustion air intake can be led from outside via "air boxes" into the fireplace. Also, the (marble) baseplate of the "styled fireplace façade" should be connected with the future parquet floor. Concrete coverings are to be installed in order to adjoin the inner wall, which was set in lime mortar almost one hundred years ago.

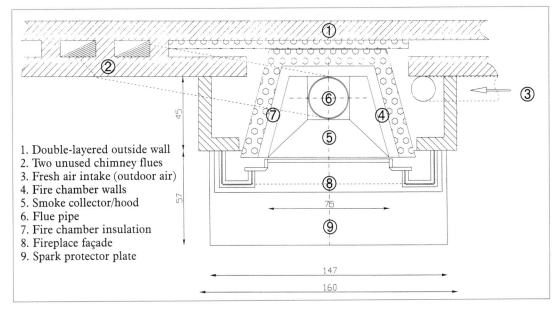

1. Double-layered outside wall
2. Two unused chimney flues
3. Fresh air intake (outdoor air)
4. Fire chamber walls
5. Smoke collector/hood
6. Flue pipe
7. Fire chamber insulation
8. Fireplace façade
9. Spark protector plate

Fig. 76: Outline drawing for the construction of the open fireplace (Fig. 75-76 by Brennpunkt Nehry & Nehry GmbH).

Fig. 77: The situation after the wall has been pierced. Here is the first foundation layer of lightweight plates for the baseplate. In the center is the hole for the fire chamber and flue pipe.

Fig. 78: Building up the outer fireplace walls.

Fig. 79: The first fireplace walls (left and right), back insulation plate, and front foundation for the baseplate.

While the drawings show a pleasant style, which was also achieved precisely, Fig. 76 already reveals the first building problems, which have to be solved on the spot.

Before the construction began, the following preparations had to be made:

—Removal of inner wall surfaces (of the double-walled house wall), so that the fireplace can be set as deeply as possible in the wall surface, and so the flue pipe (9.8 in. or 250 mm diameter) can be angled towards the two chimney flues (upper left in Fig. 76, no. 2).

—Determining whether the fresh air intake is to be placed under the fireplace floor (see Fig. 76, upper right, no. 3) or through the air space inside the outer wall.

After the wall surfaces were cleared and an air intake was made possible only through the air space between the outer walls, the builder began to prepare the foundation for the marble baseplate of the fireplace, after precisely marking the "OFF" height line, which marks the upper edge of the flooring.

Foundation and Baseplate

As already seen in Fig. 77, the builder had defined the bottom dimensions (fireplace depth and width) with lightweight plates, and in the next step, built up the outer fireplace walls (see Fig. 78). In this image the temporary supports for the inner plaster wall are still visible.

Fig. 80: With a level, the OFF height line of the present parquet is marked on the fireplace wall.

Fig. 81: The OFF line, the upper edge of the marble plate to be laid.

Fig. 82: Evenly distributed marble adhesive on the foundation plate.

Fig. 83. The builder uses wooden wedges to adjust the level of the marble plate...

Fig. 84: ...and checks the longitudinal level of the marble plate...

Fig. 85: ...until the upper edge is absolutely even with the OFF line.

In further work, additional piercing had to be carried out in order to prepare the two chimney flues for the later connection of the fireplace flue pipe. And since the "guidelines in the building of open fireplaces" call for lining the fireplace walls with insulating materials – this is especially important for adjacent walls and chimneys – the freestanding outer wall was fitted with a plate of insulation (Fig. 79). In connection with this, the foundation for the future baseplate was finished.

Since a part of the historic parquet floor still existed at the edge of this space, the builder could mark the upper edge of this flooring on the sidewall of the outside fireplace wall, in order to determine the upper level (OFF line) of the baseplate.

As soon as the OFF line has been marked, the marble plate can be set in a bed of mortar, a special mixture that will not discolor the marble (product: Alfix/Universalfix). Evenly distributed marble adhesive on the foundation plate then forms a solid base for the builder to lay the baseplate horizontally (Fig. 82-85).

Building the Fire Chamber (Herringbone Pattern)

In the layout description for this fireplace, which had been previously discussed with the homeowners, it states: "open fireplace made with firebricks in herringbone pattern..."

For the builder, this is a clear indication of the material (firebricks) and pattern (herringbone). Fire-clay bricks (and plates) have the advantage of being heat-resistant, absorbing and reflecting heat, but they are made only in sandy colors. Every tile oven and fireplace builder works with this material when fireplaces and smoke pipes are to be built. This is the case in this example, as Fig. 86-88 show.

Fig. 86: The back wall of the fire chamber, made of firebricks.

Fig. 87: The builder smoothes the joints of the back wall with his joint trowel.

Fig. 89: The ventilator in the outside wall of the house.

Fig. 88: On the finished back wall the builder marks the vertical joint line of the left fire chamber wall.

Note that in addition to this, a fireplace should be built without an ash pit, since the wood ashes carry the glowing bed as long as possible, attaining a combustion free of pollutants. In addition, a glowing bed of wood ashes provides longer-lasting heat reflection of the "hearth fire" in the living room.

In Fig. 88, two other details should be noted: Before the brick back wall of the fire chamber, the hearth of the fire chamber (fire-clay plates) with the built-in ash pit can be seen; to the left of it is one of the two pipes for combustion air intake (the right pipe is installed to the right of the fire chamber's back wall).

Fig. 90: The fire chamber, built of lightly burned bricks.

For the air intake, the builder has set an inlet grid in the outside wall (see Fig. 89), so that fresh air can be sucked in between the inner and outer walls. With a ventilator flap installed in the fireplace hood, the air supply is regulated manually. From there, the builder installed one air duct to the left and one to the right of the fireplace (see Fig. 91, fireplace hood and air boxes).

At the beginning of this section, the problem of which material (color) should be used for the fire chamber was already noted. This question does not arise for the builder, as he used fire-clay plates or bricks for the fire chamber in order to suit the fire-protection requirements. The installation of this heat-resistant material is also the basis of the guarantee provisions in the contract.

Since the homeowner did not care for the sand-colored firebricks, the fireplace builder was asked to make the fire chamber walls of burnt-red bricks instead of yellow ones! For the builder that meant tearing out the fire chamber and beginning again – and for the homeowner, no guarantee in case of possible fire chamber damage!

Hood, Ventilator, Mantel

As described previously, a handmade hood (smoke collector) was installed in this fireplace; the hood was not mounted

Fig. 91: The hood made of welded sheet steel is over the fire chamber, while the lateral air boxes are beside it.

in ceramic felt, but rather in fire-clay/potter mortar.

In Fig. 91, not only can the hood over the fire chamber be seen, already surrounded by insulating material, but also the two lateral fresh-air boxes (see Fig. 92) that will later be covered by the marble façade. In Fig. 93, the same situation is shown after the flue pipe (9.8 in. or 25 cm diameter) has been installed.

Notice that the installation of a sheet-steel hood offers the possibility of using the reflected heat to warm the room. This "convection warming" is a gain in terms of energy, but has the disadvantage that, because of the speed of air currents, permanent particles of dust are swirled into the living room and can pollute the air.

In order to prevent this hot-air circulation, the steel hood was wrapped in mineral insulating material. This does not slow the speed of the smoke, which was advisable with this chimney combination (two separate flues). The hood measures 30 in. x 20.5 in. (76 cm x 52 cm), has a shank length of 23.6 in. (60 cm) and a flue-pipe brace with a diameter of 9.8 in. (25 cm).

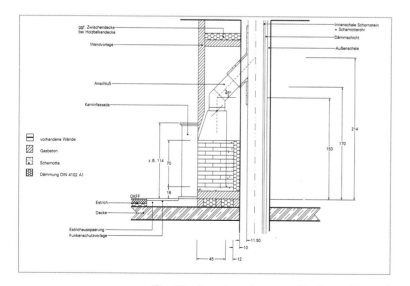

Fig. 90a: Drawing of an open fireplace with smoke collector and sheet-steel smoke pipe (drawing from Holger Reiners, *Kamine*, Munich, Callwey, 1995).

Fig. 92: A fresh-air box with a grid
opening on the fire chamber's left wall.

Fig. 93: Fireplace, hood, and smoke
pipe shortly before the final covering.

Fig. 94: The fireplace construction during
the final covering operations.

Fig. 95: The fireplace façade built up to the ceiling,
with the insulation layer visible above.

Next, the covering of 2-in. (5 cm)
lightweight plates could be built up to the
ceiling, whereby an insulation layer was
built in above the flue pipe to keep the heat
away from the ceiling.

Fig. 96: The fireplace façade.

Fig. 97: The position of the right marble column is fixed precisely to the millimeter with plaster mortar...

Fig. 98 ...

and Fig. 99: ...and the side frame parts are fitted temporarily.

Before the fireplace façade could be set, the mantel was built with two layers of modeling plaster.

Setting the Façade

In this example too, the fireplace façade consisted of various marble pieces, which were mounted on the spot. In the first step, the builder set the two marble columns on the baseplate temporarily, in order to fit the frame pieces to the sixteenth of an inch – though still temporarily as well. Only after the position of the columns was determined exactly were they "attached" with plaster mortar, in order to prevent them from moving during the subsequent work (Fig. 97).

Finally the inner frame pieces were temporarily set vertically, until the full length of the upper part of the frame was reached.

Only when the columns, the side, and upper frame members fit together without gaps are they assembled with a plaster and hemp mortar mixture. This mortar mixture is only used in certain places and is advantageous insofar as it allows for the frame members to be finely adjusted for a short period of time. A further advantage is that the entire façade can be dismantled completely, even years from now.

Using the plaster-hemp mixture at points means concretely that the frame members can be attached with this mortar to the columns, and the columns in turn with the mantel (including a caulking strip). Here we see examples:

Fig. 100: Columns and frame are fitted precisely vertically.

Fig. 101a: Hemp fibers for the plaster-hemp mortar.

Fig. 101b: The plaster-hemp mortar is mixed by hand.

Fig. 102: The mortar mixture is applied between the marble column and fireplace mantel.

Fig. 103: The upper and right frame members are attached to the column in the rear with plaster-hemp mortar.

Fig. 104: The mortar connection between the column and the upper interior frame (center).

Fig. 105: Next all the frame members are adjusted precisely, checked with the level and, if necessary, carefully corrected.

Only when the columns have been attached to the inner frame members "hairbreadth close," including the gently arched upper frame member, can the marble mantelpiece be set. First it must be noted how the bonding between the marble façade and the brick fire chamber has been made. Only

heat-resistant and flexible materials, such as ceramic felt, ceramic paste, quick-setting mortar, and non-flammable flexible strips are suitable, as well as commercial potter's/stove-builder's mortar. In this example, the space between the upper arched frame, which is attached directly to the sheet-steel

Fig. 106: The open fireplace before the marble mantelpiece is installed.

Fig. 107: The caulking strip "stuck on" between the upper marble frame and the sheet-steel hood (seen from above and to the side).

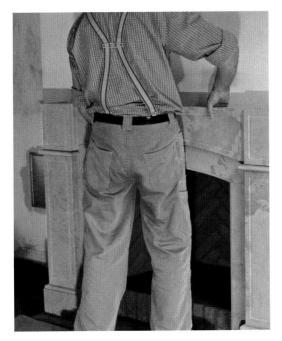

Fig. 108: The fireplace builder sets the mantelpiece on the columns and frame construction…

Fig. 109: …later to be completed with a mantel plate.

hood of the fireplace, is filled with a non-flammable flexible strip, which the builder attaches with the already mentioned plaster-hemp mortar and then covers with quick-setting mortar (Fig. 107). Only when all attachments to the fireplace are made airtight and sealed can the upper part of the fireplace façade, and the mantelpiece be set horizontally and completed with the finishing mantel plate. The already mentioned mortar mixture is used here too, and is never visible from outside.

Fig. 110. The open fireplace in the midst of the library.

Flames Behind Glass:

Fireplaces in

Modern Style

Fireplace 4:

Classic Design with a Window: A Fireplace for Two Rooms

Fig. 111: The open fireplace with styled façade and see-through window.

A Fireplace for Two Rooms?

After a rundown 19th-century villa had been renovated stylishly and laboriously over the years by the parents who occupied the ground floor of the house, their recently-married son and his wife decided to redecorate their own dwelling in the upper floor according to their own tastes. Among their ideas was the wish for an open fireplace with a styled façade of marble. Since the young lady was expecting a baby, the fire was to be protected by a glass panel.

After the first consultations and in intensive discussions with the fireplace builder, they developed the idea of building a fireplace that could be seen from two sides. This variation was possible because the fireplace could be set into an inside wall.

Fig. 112: The renovated 19th-century two-family house.

Drawings to Help You Decide

The decision to construct a special fireplace was eased when the potential customers were given drawings that showed the fireplace they wanted in a real living area, as shown in this example (Fig. 113-116).

Preliminary Work

on the Window

In the layout description that was discussed with the homeowners and builder before the work started, these points, among others, were listed:

—Make the cut through the wall.
—Build the concrete lintel.

—Remove old asphalt pavement.
—Install a steel plate (0.25 in. or 6 mm) on the old wooden floor.
—Lay a cement surface (2 in. or 50 mm) horizontally on the steel plate.
—Install a flue pipe (fox) to the chimney.
—Install an air intake through the outside wall, with manually adjustable air flap (6 in. or 150 mm diameter), and set it in masonry.

A "see-through prefabricated fireplace" made by the Spartheim firm, with a sliding glass door in the living room and an opening glass door in the reading room. A styled marble façade was wanted for the living room. A slim frame of emerald-pearl granite strips was to give the

Fig. 113: The drawing shows the fireplace in the living room. (Drawings 113-116 by Brennpunkt Nehry & Nehry GmbH)

Fig. 114: View of the fireplace in the informal reading room.

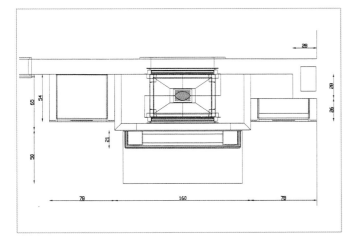

Fig. 115: The "see-through fireplace" with façade, seen from above.

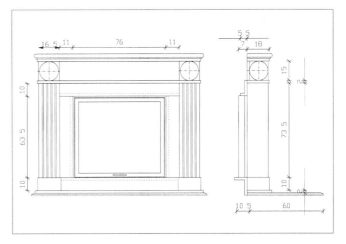

Fig. 116: Front and side views of the marble façade.

Fig. 117: The window in the wall,
with masonry lintel.

Fig. 118: The window with insulation plates and
first façade, with a vent opening at lower left.

glass-protected fire that simplicity that was part of the young couple's lifestyle in the reading room.

Piercing the Wall

and Beginning the Fireplace

Besides the milieu drawings (Fig. 113-114), the builder also had scale drawings (Fig. 115-116) and thus could begin with the preliminary work.

After the wall had been pierced, the lintel was installed, the new concrete layer was formed, and the inside surfaces of the "window" were fitted with insulation plates in order to prevent the wall and lintel from being exposed to too much heat (Fig. 118).

Then the builder began to form the fireplace mantel with lightweight plates (2 in. or 5 cm thick). And since the fireplace was to provide not only reflected warmth but also convection warmth, it was necessary to leave two openings in the lower part of the mantel. Through these openings, cooler room air would be sucked in when

the fire was on, and be given off into the room above the fireplace when warmed (see Fig. 122).

Only after the preliminary work was done could the heavy unit be set horizontally and vertically (Fig. 119-120).

Masonry for the Fireplace Unit

Before the fireplace façade in the living room could be extended to the ceiling, the flue pipes from the prefabricated unit had to be extended to the chimney and sealed. And since the cross-section form of the chimney allowed only one smoke pipe with a diameter of 7 in. (180 mm), it was necessary to install a reducing piece between the fireplace pipe (7.8 in. or 200 mm diameter) and the adjoining flue pipe (7 in. or 180 mm diameter).

For the construction of the fireplace mantel, only lightweight plates (Ytong) 2 in. (5 cm) thick were used, attached to each other with a special adhesive. In Fig. 122, the lower part of the fireplace façade is shown before plastering. A few details may be noted here:

Fig. 119: The fireplace unit in the wall perforation, with its glass wall raised.

Fig. 120: The back of the fireplace unit, with warm air openings in the hood.

—Insulation plates were integrated into the mantel to the left, right, and above the fireplace unit to ward off future heat.
—In the upper part of the picture, the two hot-air openings that were covered by a layer of insulation can be seen.

This design equals the function of a hot-air tile oven, which produces not only radiating heat but also warms the room air (convection warming). Instead of a tile mantel, which would have been much more costly, the couple decided on a building material that could be plastered to achieve a smooth background.

Fig. 121: The reducing section has been installed between the hood and the smoke pipe.

Fig. 122: The fireplace mantel of lightweight plates, with two hot-air openings (above the center).

Since the location of the fireplace was not right beside the chimney, it was necessary to pipe the smoke from the fireplace to the chimney at a right angle below the ceiling. This steel-pipe link needed to be surrounded on all sides with insulation plates and an opening left for the cleaning hatch (Fig. 123, upper right). And because the ceiling over the fireplace was to be protected from fire, the flue pipe was also wrapped in insulating material (Fig. 123).

Plastering the Mantel

When the three-sided fireplace mantel has been set vertically from floor to ceiling and the last corrections have been made, the builder attaches plaster frames (sometimes also called corner protectors) at the corners.

These plaster frames are put on vertically and not only make plastering easier, but also, as the second term suggests, prevent damage to the plastered corner areas.

It is simplest to attach the frames with ceiling nails; another possibility is to set the frame strip in mortar and place it vertically.

Regardless of how the frames are attached, the builder first checks to see if the mantel was walled up vertically. And since there are sometimes small, barely visible depressions, they can be evened up with the

Fig. 123: The fireplace mantel before plastering. Above, the flue pipe is being insulated; to the right is the connection to the chimney with a cleaning hatch.

Fig. 124: The builder attaches the vertical plaster frames with ceiling nails in the upper...

Fig. 125: ...and lower areas of the fireplace edges.

Fig. 126: A sheet of armament fabric is applied to stabilize the modeling plaster.

plaster frames and the modeling plaster to be applied later. A long bar, similar to a ruler, is vital here.

As soon as the plastering and corner-protecting frames are attached vertically, the armament fabric is laid on the full surface and likewise temporarily fastened with ceiling nails (Fig. 126). The Armierung fabric can also be laid in a previously spread bed of mortar.

To finish this step, the frames for the hot-air grids (above and below) were mounted *before* the plastering, and it was necessary that their outer edges matched those of the plaster frames. The armament fabric also had to be cut away from these openings in advance (Fig. 127) to make a flat, even layer of plaster.

The builder then placed all the horizontal and vertical strips and frames in the modeling plaster, which was mixed to a consistency (Fig. 128) that did not run from the trowel and could be worked quickly.

Fig. 127: After the armament fabric is "stuck on" with plaster mortar, the builder removes the fabric from the hot-air openings.

Fig. 128: The master builder mixes the modeling plaster for the first application.

Fig. 129: The first layer of modeling plaster is pressed onto the armament fabric and smoothed with a trowel.

Fig. 130: Smoothing the second layer of mortar with a bar from below...

Fig. 131: ...to the ceiling, whereby the plaster frames are a big help.

Fig. 132: All the surfaces of the mantel are smoothed with the rubber trowel.

Because the plaster layer can be up to 0.4 in. (10 mm) thick, the first layer of mortar is pressed into the armament fabric and smoothed with the smoothing trowel (Fig. 129). Only when the second layer of mortar has been spread with the trowel will it be "smoothed down" with a bar to form a uniform surface.

The last uneven spots are then evened up and smoothed before all the surfaces of the fireplace mantel are finally smoothed with a rubber trowel. This is a process that only experienced stove and fireplace builders can carry out (Fig. 132).

Mounting the Marble Façade

For the fireplace and oven builder, the individual tiles for the oven or the individual parts of a fireplace façade, made of finely polished natural stone (such as marble or granite), are the materials that he handles with particular care.

Baseplate and Console

Since the carpet in the living room was to remain while the fireplace was built, it was necessary to cut the piece under the baseplate off to guarantee the stability of the

fireplace coating. For this, the baseplate had to be laid on the carpet, centered with the prefabricated fireplace, and the cutting angles cut (Fig. 133). Then the natural-stone adhesive could be applied and the baseplate laid horizontally on the adhesive (Fig. 134-137) with wooden wedges to help make the final corrections.

Fig. 134: The free floor surface is covered with marble adhesive…

Fig. 133: The carpet is cut away at the corners of the baseplate.

Fig. 135: …and the baseplate is laid horizontally.

Fig. 136: Checking the horizontal position of the baseplate.

Fig. 137: Final corrections are made with wooden wedges.

Fig. 138: The marble console is covered with adhesive…

Fig. 139: …and set horizontally on the baseplate.

Fig. 140: The upright fireplace columns are then set loosely on the console to check the precise measurements of the frame parts.

Fig. 141: Checking the vertical position of the right column.

After the baseplate was adjusted horizontally and the mortar had set sufficiently to bear a load, the console for the two upright columns was laid. Here too, the builder used the marble adhesive already mentioned.

Setting Uprights and Frame

Experienced oven and fireplace builders who combine pre-cut parts of a fireplace façade know with what concentration this work needs to be done.

Therefore the fireplace builder decided at first to determine the positions of the two upright columns on the console exactly, to be sure that the inner frame members would fit together precisely (Fig. 140). For a precise fit it was also necessary to check the vertical position of each column (Fig. 141) and adjust it with very thin pieces of sheet lead.

As soon as all the dimensions were determined and marked, the columns were removed and the lower part of the frame was laid in natural-stone mortar. To stabilize these lower parts of the inner frame members, lime-sandstones were laid in mortar between the console and the prefabricated fireplace unit to prevent tipping.

After these preparations were finished, the job of setting the upright marble columns could begin, with very thin lead sheets used to balance them perfectly (Fig. 146).

Fig. 142: With pieces of sheet lead hammered very thin...

Fig. 143: ...the builder adjusts the vertical position of the columns.

Fig. 144: The lower frame part of the fireplace façade is set precisely in natural-stone mortar.

Fig. 145: The fireplace façade after the baseplate, console, and lower frame member have been installed.

Fig. 146: The master builder adjusts the vertical position of the left column with hand-hammered pieces of lead.

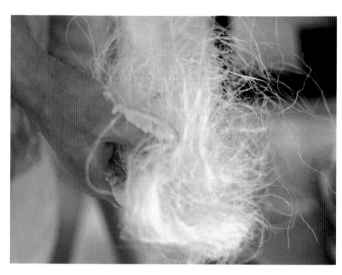

Fig. 147: The hemp fibers before being mixed with plaster.

Fig. 148: The clumps of plaster are a helpful mortar mixture for attaching columns, frame parts, and mantel together.

Fig. 149: The builder carefully attaches the upper end of the column and the mantel with plaster-hemp mortar.

Fig. 150: The column-linking marble mantel-piece shortly before being set.

Fig. 151: The last distance corrections are made to the set mantelpiece.

Fig. 152: All joints are filled with natural stone adhesive and smoothed. At the lower right is the fresh air duct next to the chimney.

Fig. 153: The mantelpiece is set carefully in natural-stone mortar. Above the fireplace are the closed hot-air openings.

Only when both columns and the side frame members that go with them were firmly set in plaster was the mortar mixture of plaster and hemp made, as was described in the previous chapter. It should be noted that the builder had to let a clump of mortar fall into the column where he could not reach by hand, so that the marble parts would be attached solidly to the console and mantel at the bottom (Fig. 148-149).

Setting the Mantel

and Mantelpiece

Setting the mantelpiece ranks among the most tense moments in building a fireplace. Up to this point, all the inner rame members and columns have been set precisely. And since the quick-setting mortar mixture scarcely allows for horizontal or vertical adjustments, the builder relies on his previous work. It gives him the assur-ance that the mantelpiece, the "lintel" of the fireplace façade, will fit exactly, as happened in this instance (Fig. 150-151).

Before the upper marble plate (mantel plate) could be laid, the last cosmetic touches were to be made to the marble pieces already in place. All the joints between the marble pieces also had to be filled with natural-stone adhesive then smoothed, and the attachment areas for the mantelpiece also had to be spread with the same adhesive. Only then could the mantelpiece be set in the mortar (Fig. 152-153). In Fig. 152, 153, and 154, the fresh air duct, which brings outside air to the fire chamber of the fireplace as soon as a fire is lit, can be seen at the lower right. A flexible aluminum pipe is well suited for this. And since not only the fresh air duct, but also a cleaning hatch for the chimney had to be built in, considerable breaking and boring had to be done, but any experienced oven or fireplace builder could do them.

Fig. 154: The fireplace shortly before the work is done. At the lower right, the covering of the fresh air duct is still missing.

Fig. 155: The fresh air duct to the left and the cleaning hatch with condensed water drain to the right in the outside wall.

The Façade in

the Reading Room

Up to now, only the fireplace construction in the future living room has been documented, without dealing with the work on the opposite side of the fireplace. This will be described here only in brief, as some steps in the work will be repeated.

This reduction becomes clear when one looks back at the drawing (Fig. 114) in which the fireplace is surrounded by a simple frame.

Fig. 156: The prefabricated fireplace in the pierced wall, with the flue-pipe connector.

Fig. 157: Preparatory work for the final application of plaster. In the center is the first insulating plate.

Fig. 158: The surface to be plastered alongside and above the fireplace window, with the hot-air opening visible above.

Fig. 159: The first layer of plaster for the armament fabric.

Fig. 160: Fitting the armament fabric.

Fig. 161: Smoothing the second layer of plaster with the trowel.

Fig. 162: The last uneven spots are smoothed with the rubber trowel.

In the next illustrations, Fig. 156 to 163, forming the fireplace façade in the future reading and relaxing room is described briefly. The starting point was piercing the wall and placing the fireplace unit, which was placed so that the window frame projected about .6 in. (15 mm). This equaled the medium thickness of the plaster to be applied. The frame and plaster were to be almost even.

Heat Insulation and Plastering

Whenever a wall is pierced, even if it is cut in advance with an angle-cutter, flakes of plaster break off the wall and have to be filled in before the final modeling plaster can be made flat.

Thus the edges of the wall opening were first fitted with insulating material and the joint angles evened with heat-resistant modeling plaster (Fig. 157). Before that, the builder began to seal the fireplace surface above the fire chamber with insulation plates, which later became plaster carriers. Tip: All insulation plates were laid with heat-resistant quick-setting mortar.

If one compares Fig. 158 with Fig. 156, it becomes clear why the building material in this area must be protected from the heat of future fireplace fires. In addition, this "heat-deflecting" design lets the thermally induced cooler room air warm up faster. As soon as the joint surfaces were sealed, the builder decided to apply the armament fabric for the modeling plaster "wet-in-wet." The first plaster layer had to be applied very quickly (Fig. 159) to attach the fabric (Fig. 160) and press it in with a trowel (Fig. 161). Finally, all plastered fireplace surfaces were prepared with the rubber trowel for the last artistic work.

Fig. 163: The fireplace window with hot-air opening and plastered wall surface.

Fireplace 5:

A Blend of Steel and Glass

Architecture and

Fireplace Design

An architect built his dream house of concrete, steel, highly browned bricks, pre-patinaed copper plate, and lots and lots of glass for daylight in the rooms.

Since these materials were combined in a building style reminiscent of classic Bauhaus architecture, with its experimentation in new forms and colors, the design of the "open" fireplace was transformed into a hearth fire behind a trapezoid-shaped lifting glass panel!

Fig. 165: The southwest façade of the house after the fireplace was installed.

Fig. 164: The trapezoidal fireplace with colorful mantel.

Surface and

Structure Drawings

The geometric shape of this fireplace is clear in Fig. 166, 167, and 168. The fireplace consists of a masonry foundation at seat level, topped by the trapezoidal fireplace unit with a glass panel that slides up, and finished with a double-walled stainless steel chimney with an interior diameter of 8 in. (20 cm).

The stainless steel chimney rises through two floors. The upper floor is like a "terrace in a room," and the stainless steel column that rises through it acts as a decorative element. In Fig. 167 the design of the fireplace is even clearer: the hearth repeats the trapezoidal form of the prefabricated unit and simultaneously links the fireplace to the two-story windows on either side. According to the ground plan, it was noted in the raw building phase that the base area was not to be fitted with "floating concrete" (on insulation plates), but rather with a supporting layer of concrete. A detailed drawing was made available to the builders before the building firm began its work.

Tip: Whoever is interested in having an open or enclosed fireplace built should make sure that the builder contacts the local building inspector during the planning phase to obtain clearance in advance! See also the *Building and Assembly Tips* section of this book.

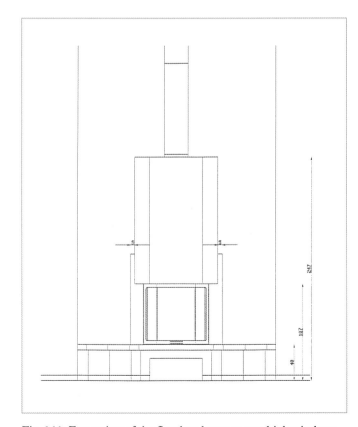

Fig. 166: Front view of the fireplace between two high windows. (Fig. 166-168: Brennpunkt Nehry & Nehry GmbH)

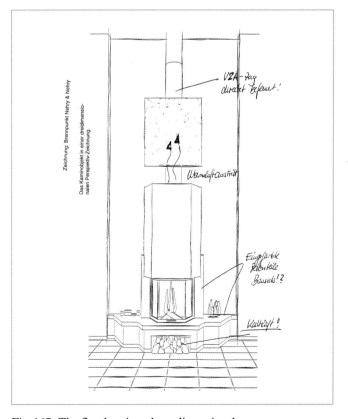

Fig. 167: The fireplace in a three-dimensional perspective drawing.

1. Prefabricated fireplace unit
2. Flue pipe (inset)
3. Stainless steel chimney
4. Hot air openings
5. Carrier frame for façade
6. Base

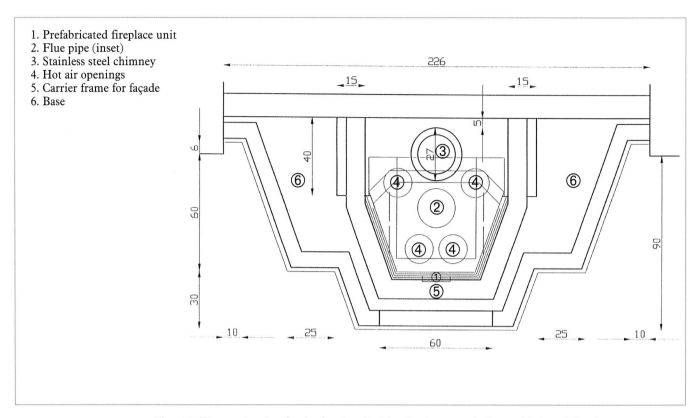

Fig. 168: The top drawing for the fireplace builder: In the center is the prefabricated fireplace with flue-pipe opening and chimney; beside and before it are the hot air openings.

Building the Base

Before the fireplace unit could be set in place, three steps had to be taken:
—Mounting the adjustable fresh-air intake flap on the inside of the outer wall.
—Mounting a 3.2-in. (80 mm) thick insulation plate on the inside of the outer wall.
—Laying out the masonry base.

Because construction of the base could begin only after the fireplace unit was set horizontally and vertically and the fresh-air flap was attached, there was enough time to cut the individual lightweight plates precisely and – according to plan – set them in mortar.

Better understanding of the mounting of the fireplace unit can be gained from Fig. 170.

Fig. 169: Building the base for the fireplace unit. The stainless steel chimney is already installed above; below it is the flue pipe of the fireplace unit.

1. Prefabricated fireplace unit
2. Convection space
3. Smoke flap (to be mounted on building side)
4. Fresh air flap
5. Carrier frame for façade
6. Flue pipe to chimney
7. Insulation around smoke pipe
8. Heated room air
9. Hot-air exit
10. Air exit into room
11. Outside air intake (fresh air)
12. Floor
13. Wall (with masonry projection 17 and Daemmung 24)
14. Ceiling
15. Concrete slab
16. Mineral building material
18. Fireplace apron (mantel)
19. Extension joint
20. Base covering
21. Omitted
22. Fender and connection with floor
23. Lower heat shield
24. Side and back heat shields
25. Upper heat shield. Data from instructions by Sablux AG, Switzerland

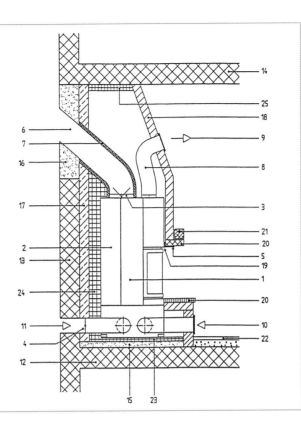

Fig. 170: Drawing for the construction of an open fireplace with a prefabricated fireplace unit. (Drawing: Sablux AG, Bachenbülach, Switzerland)

Fig. 171: The trapezoidal fireplace unit with masonry base and room air opening below the unit.

Fig. 172: After the base is built, the builder installs the side columns.

Turning aside from this schematic drawing, we must add that the flue pipe of the fireplace unit had to be connected to the stainless steel chimney installed in the room, a direct process that had to be cleared with the building inspector.

To build the foundation, erected and covered exclusively with 2 in. (5 cm) thick lightweight plates, it can be added that an opening was left on the front side (see Fig. 166, 167 and 170a) as a room air intake and hot air exit (Fig. 170, # 9). In Fig. 171, the knob with which the fresh air supply is regulated can be seen next to the "room air opening."

Before the furnace façade could be built, the side "frame pillars" wanted by the homeowner had to be installed, later to be covered with cobalt blue glazed tiles (Fig. 165, 172).

The Fireplace Façade

The façade of the upper part of the fireplace unit (see Fig. 165) could be built only after a carrier frame was installed. This trapezoidal frame – of L-iron – can bear the weight of the façade of 0.8 in. (2 cm) reinforced plaster plates, but only permanently if it is solidly anchored.

Therefore it was connected to the outer wall on both sides – resting on the back columns. Connected means that two appropriately small holes were cut in the outer wall, in which the two ends of the frame were set and attached with reinforced plaster mortar.

To firmly bear the future weight of the fireplace mantel in the front, above the fire chamber, a thin steel strip was attached to the carrier frame and the upper edge of the unit.

Only after this carrier frame was anchored horizontally could work on the façade begin. Reinforced plaster plates are especially suitable because they resist heat and are easy to set as long as an experienced furnace builder does the job (see Fig. 173-178).

Fig. 173: The carrier frame above the fire chamber must fit precisely.

Fig. 174: Covering the upper part of the fireplace unit. In the center is the vertically mounted steel strip.

Fig. 175: The fireplace structure after the side covering plates have been installed vertically.

Fig. 176: The fireplace seen from the same angle in Fig. 165.

Fig. 177: Vertical setting of the front fireplace covering.

Fig. 178: Vertical installation of the upper fireplace covering, after the flue pipe has been attached to the stainless steel chimney.

Fig. 179: The fireplace hood is covered with an insulation plate.

These steps also included wrapping the upper fireplace covering with a layer of heat insulation. Aside from the fact that this insulation is required for fire safety, it also allows optimal warming in the room-air chamber under the fireplace. In Fig. 179, this step is prepared for. The final covering is made of a reinforced plaster plate cut to fit. Here too, the fire-resistant adhesive was adequate.

Armament Fabric

and First Plaster Layer

As soon as the fireplace hood, also called the fireplace mantel, was completed, the plastering could begin. To avoid future cracks that might form because of the convection heat (inside the mantel), the first plaster layer was covered with armament fabric.

Fig. 180: The builder attaches the armament fabric on the already applied "plaster surfaces" ...

Fig. 181: ...and applies the first layer of plaster with a smoothing trowel.

Fig. 182: Armament fabric and plaster on the lower mantel, above the fire chamber.

Fig. 183: Vertical installation of the plaster frames on the right side of the mantel.

Fig. 184: The corner brace set vertically in quick-setting mortar above the carrier frame; at the right center the armament fabric can be seen.

Fig. 185: The builder applies the second crude plaster layer with a trowel...

Fig. 186: ...and spreads it evenly on the surface between the corner braces.

Fig. 187: The fireplace after the plastering is finished.

Fig. 188: Laying the cut and polished hearthstones.

Fig. 189: The open fireplace in the middle of the
south wall, after the hearthstones have been laid.

Fig. 189a: The "open fireplace" with unpainted hood.

Instead of attaching this stabilizing fabric mechanically (such as with nails), the builder set this armament in quickly applied plaster (Fig. 180); then the plaster could be spread on the whole surface and smoothed.

Corner Braces

and Second Plaster Layer

One of the builder's architectonic ideas was to form the angles of the trapezoidal fireplace mantel as clearly visible vertical lines. For this, corner braces or plaster frames are mounted vertically for this purpose before the second plaster layer is applied.

As soon as all the vertical plaster frames are attached to the mantel, the second and last layer of plaster, 0.3 in. to 0.4 in. (8mm to 10 mm) thick, is applied with a smoothing trowel (Fig. 185) and then spread evenly on the surface with a plaster frame bar (Fig. 186). As soon as the plaster has begun to set, it is smoothed permanently with a felt or rubber trowel.

Granite and Color

If one compares the picture at the beginning of this chapter (Fig. 164) with Fig. 187, it becomes clear that the builder has finished his part of the work, but that other artisans can add much to the final design of this fireplace object. Specialists who know the colors of various granites and other types of stone applied very dark hearthstones of South African stone (Fig. 188, 189) to the hearth. Another part of the design concept was the decor of the fireplace hood and the two adjoining wall surfaces as individual color phenomena: a warm contrast to steel, glass, and granite.

Fig. 190: The hood of the fireplace, painted with a wiping technique.

Fireplace 6:

Fire Behind Curved Glass

Old House

Renovation and New Fireplace

Experienced artisans know what it means when a two-family house, built at the beginning of the 20th century and protected as a historic site, must be renovated from the ground up.

Renovating an old house is hard work, all the more so as new standards define the desire for living comfort and aesthetics.

Fig. 191: The last work on the curved fireplace.

Fig. 192: The "old" two-family house with bay windows in the alcove area.

It is also thus in fireplace building when an old chimney is to carry off the smoke of an open fireplace fire safely into the open air. In case the dimensions of the decades-old chimney flue are too small for an "open fire," a fireplace fitted with a fire-chamber door is recommended.

Sometimes old houses have the advantage of chimneys with two flues that, coupled together, allow a fireplace connection acceptable to the local building inspector.

Chimney and Foundation

In the description of this fireplace project, the builder was instructed to remove the parquet floor in the fireplace area and install a strong foundation.

In addition, the two available chimney flues should be combined to guarantee the functional capability of the fireplace. The air intake (air for combustion) should come in through the cellar (fresh air pipe diameter 8 cm or 20 cm). Before the parquet floor in the future fireplace area could be removed, the chimney flues had to be located.

Fig. 194: The opened chimney flues: at left is the unused one, at right is the one used many years ago.

Fig. 195: Sawing away the parquet floor for the fireplace foundation.

Fig. 193: The fireplace builder breaches the two chimney flues for the fireplace connections.

Fig. 196: The concrete foundation for the fireplace unit, with the fresh-air intake pipe at left.

Only when the chimney connection area is open can the curved line for the foundation be marked precisely on the parquet and sawn out (Fig. 195.)

Installing the

Fireplace and Foundation

Only when the concrete foundation can bear a load and the chimney wall has been fitted with insulation plates, can the fireplace unit, almost 6.6 ft. (2 m) high, be set vertically and horizontally (it weighs ca. 800 lb. or 400 kg!). In Fig. 197 it is clear that this job should be performed by at least two people.

In Fig. 197 the heat insulation behind the fireplace unit and the high opening to the chimney can also be seen. A few notes: to assure optimal smoke exhaust, the brickwork between the two flues was removed for about 19.7 in. (50 cm) for better circulation.

Before the builder could begin to build the foundation, all the outlines had to be marked precisely. They were based on two drawings. One of them (Fig. 199) shows the future fireplace in the living-room milieu; the other includes all the rounded lines, including the fireplace unit, the foundation, and the glass plate that is to be installed in front of the fireplace (Fig. 200).

Fig. 197: Setting the prefabricated fireplace unit on the concrete foundation.

Fig. 198: Horizontal and vertical adjustment of the fireplace unit; the fresh and room air openings can be seen at the lower right.

Fig. 199: Drawing of the semicircular fireplace to be built (Drawings 199 and 200 by Brennpunkt Nehry & Nehry GmbH).

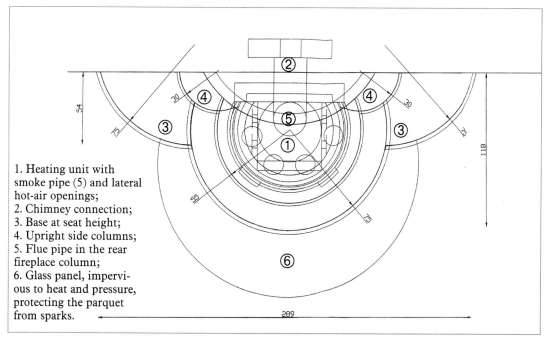

1. Heating unit with smoke pipe (5) and lateral hot-air openings;
2. Chimney connection;
3. Base at seat height;
4. Upright side columns;
5. Flue pipe in the rear fireplace column;
6. Glass panel, impervious to heat and pressure, protecting the parquet from sparks.

Fig. 200: Top view of the numerous sections of the base and columns.

Fig. 201: The builder sets the flexible lamella-like wall of the base, and stabilizes it inside with quick-setting mortar...

Fig. 202: ...adjusting its vertical position with a level.

Fig. 203: Height correction of the foundation wall using wooden wedges.

Fig. 204: The lower foundation surface before being covered with sandstone plates.

After marking the outlines on the concrete foundation and the parquet, the builder began the vertical construction of the base. In turning the curved lines into a stable vertical element, he used a lamella-like, and thus flexible, reinforced plaster form (Fig. 201) cut to size on the site.

To define the base height (15 in. or 38 cm without covering plates) as a horizontal surface, height corrections with wooden wedges were required, as every fireplace and oven builder knows, as a means of fine adjustment.

Before the 15-in. (38 cm) base was covered with three precut 1.6-in. (4 cm) thick sandstone plates, the flue pipe (9.8 in. or 25 cm diameter) with the choke flap had to be attached to the double-flue chimney. For fire-protection reasons, the heat insulation was completed behind the fireplace (see Fig. 206).

Building the

Columns and Façade

In Fig. 191, (page 80) the right column, fireplace mantel, and upper fireplace pillar can be seen clearly. For technical comprehension, one can also note Fig. 200 (out

Fig. 205: Fitting the central sandstone baseplate; the flue pipe can be seen in place above.

Fig. 206: The installed smoke pipe and the first column to the right of the fireplace unit.

Fig. 207: Pillar construction and hood covering (with choke handle) on the left side of the fireplace.

Fig. 208: The builder sets the upper rear covering, behind which is the flue pipe's connection to the chimney.

line drawing) to better understand the design.

Flexible reinforced plaster forms were set in quick-setting mortar and finally attached, just as they were for the base construction. In Fig. 206, the column to the

Fig. 209: The builder begins to apply the first layer of plaster...

right of the fireplace unit and its temporary cover can be seen; at the lower right is a part of the base covered with sandstone.

To cover the hood of the fireplace unit, the carrier frame had to be mounted first; it is delivered as part of the set and carries the weight of the covering securely. In addition, the handle of the choke flap in the smoke pipe had to be mounted in the covering of the fireplace hood (upper left).

After the hood was covered with a sandstone plate cut exactly to fit, the builder could begin on the upper rear column. The sandstone plate was not only cut precisely, but also fitted with the prescribed round hot-air opening.

In Fig. 207, it can be seen that the construction of the hood covering was temporarily halted. This was done to prevent crack formation in the freshly set fireplace mantel.

Only when this elliptical upper fireplace covering is finally covered with an insulation plate and a sandstone plate can the builder prepare for the last step of the work.

Fig. 210: ...into which the armament fabric is pressed with the smoothing trowel.

Plaster and Armament Fabric

Two coats of plaster were necessary for this fireplace. The first layer consisted of an armament plaster (made by Rath), which was applied to the full surface. Then the armament fabric could be pressed "wet-in-wet" into the fresh plaster.

Only when the armament plaster has set can the final plaster be applied and spread evenly with a handmade plastering tool. The last fine details, such as wiping surface structures, can be made only by the professional fireplace builder.

Fig. 211: The last fine details of the almost-finished fireplace are made with a rubber trowel.

Open Fireplaces in Free Style

Fireplace 7:

Warm Sculpture in White

In the Beginning

there was the Model

The proprietor of this fireplace project decided on a unique form and found in Gery and Erno Wiedenmann the right planning partners. Fireplace planning talks took place on the isolated and building-free property. Outline and cutaway drawings for the future one-family house were the basis for a handmade model in 1:10 scale (9.8 in. or 25 cm high, room height 8 ft. or 250 cm).

The fireplace shape suited the owner's sense of style and form, and was based on the form of flames.

Fig. 212: The sculptured fireplace on the ground floor. (Photo: Chiemton)

Fig. 213: The fireplace model with the steps to the second floor.

Fresh Air Vent and Base

Not only are the stairway to the upper floor and the chimney next to it built expressly for the open fireplace, shown in Fig. 214, but so are four flexible aluminum pipes (lower left), which are to supply the furnace with fresh air.

These fresh air ducts (3.9 in. or 10 cm diameter) were laid from the ventilated cellar to the ground floor before work on the fireplace began. But this required that the oven and fireplace builder had previously marked the outlines of the fireplace so that the break through the cellar ceiling could be made precisely.

And with the outlines, the foundation began to take form. But how do you outline the base of a fireplace of which only a model and no scale drawings, no straight lines, and no precise angle exist as a starting point?

Here an experienced fireplace and oven builder who did not need straight lines, precise angles, or a level as the basis of his work, but who was capable of converting the forms

and masses of the model fireplace into the full-sized, real thing was needed.

Along with this, the shape of the foundation, the fireplace opening, and the outer shape of the fireplace were laid out only with

Fig. 214: The building site before work on the fireplace begins.

Fig. 215: Setting the foundation with perforated bricks. The four fresh air ducts are at right.

Fig. 216: The first layer of the base with the bent fresh-air ducts.

Fig. 217: After the base's height is reached, the inner structure is built up to the same height.

the help of a bent ruler. With this simple method, the outer shape of the foundation could be defined and marked, while the builder always kept one eye on the model.

Since the fresh air ducts were to be laid adjacent to the future fire chamber, this was kept in mind while the foundation was built. In our example, the fresh air intakes were to be installed on the left and right sides of the fire chamber. In Fig. 217, the builder is bending the ducts on the left and right edges of the foundation before building up the foundation surface with large perforated bricks. Note that the rim of the base was built "in plumb" without a level!

Fig. 218: Laying out the firebricks in fire-resistant mortar, forming a curved line.

Fig. 219: The fire chamber floor after the second level of bricks was laid, with one of the fresh air ducts at left.

Fig. 220: The symmetrically bent ruler is checked for height with another and corrected to about 23.6 in. (60 cm).

Fig. 221: The frame construction of the fire chamber opening begins, guided by the bent ruler.

Building the Fire Chamber

The Fire Chamber Basin

Since the floor of the fire chamber was also to represent the free, organic form of the fireplace, the builder laid the firebricks in fire-resistant mortar in a basin shape.

After the second row of bricks was laid, all the joints were filled evenly with fireplace mortar (Fig. 219) before the asymmetrical fire chamber opening was shaped with a bent ruler.

The Asymmetrical

Fireplace Opening

According to the dictionary definition, asymmetry means "lack of symmetry, unevenness." Unevenness is exactly the concept of this fireplace's design (beginning with the outline, the shape of the base, and the layout of the fire chamber floor), which was continued in the formation of the fire chamber opening. For this phase too, the "bent" ruler was an unusual aid (see Fig. 220).

After these first steps and last corrections – always with one eye on the model to make sure that the fragmented arc did

not fall apart under the weight of the firebricks, the builder braced the ruler with loosely piled perforated bricks, as shown in Fig. 224.

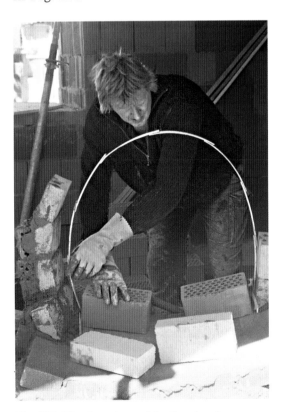

Fig. 222: The first phase of the fire chamber construction, with the bent ruler in the center. The arch is being corrected for the last time.

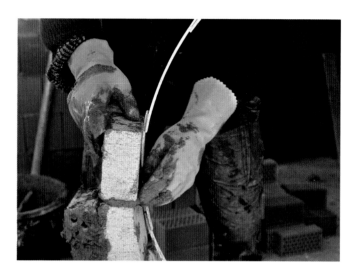

Fig. 223: Working on the details of the arch construction.

Fig. 224: The arch was built with the help of loosely stacked perforated bricks.

Fig. 225: The arch of the fireplace opening; above is the chimney opening for the fireplace. In the background is the stairway to the upper floor.

Building the Fire Chamber

and Fresh Air Openings

During the time period in which the arch construction set and hardened in order to be load-bearing later on, the builder finished the basin-like floor of the fire chamber. He began by building the fire chamber, for which only firebricks set at angles in fireplace mortar were used.

Since the fresh air ducts from the cellar were to be right next to the future fire, openings were planned in the side (left and right) fire chamber walls. In Fig. 227 the right-side opening for fresh air supply (6 in. x 6 in. or 15 cm x 15 cm) can be seen.

Fig. 226: The arch and the finished fire chamber floor.

Fig. 228: The base and first fire chamber wall with the fresh air opening, and the arch of the fireplace opening to the rear.

Fig. 227: The fireplace opening with the fire chamber wall and fresh air opening.

Fig. 229: The arch and fire chamber wall with fresh air opening (right center).

Fig. 230: The left fresh air opening near the arch.

Fig. 231: The arched fire chamber construction (partly supported). At left, the builder connects the fireplace opening to the mantel.

Fig. 232: The crudely plastered fireplace opening with the top partly supported.

After the second wall of bricks set on end was built, the builder began to set all the other firebricks in arcs to repeat the form of the model. Since the quick-setting mortar only held the bricks set at angles, boards were used to support the construction in the upper part of the fire chamber. While this construction dried and the quick-setting mortar set, the fireplace opening was completed as in the model (Fig. 231).

To equal the form of the model and block off the fresh air ducts to the outside, the builder built a layer of bricks in the front of the fire chamber; it became progressively thinner as it was built upward. For this construction, heat-resistant quick-setting mortar was used (Fig. 233).

With this quick-setting mortar the fireplace mantel was then plastered and the final shape prepared, although the upper part of the fire chamber was not yet finished.

Fig. 233: Covering the fresh air intake and shaping the fireplace sculpture.

Fig. 234: The mantel is coated with heat-resistant quick-setting mortar, and the final shape is prepared.

Fig. 235: The crudely plastered fireplace, with the stairs to the upper floor in the background.

Fig. 236: The fireplace shape before the fire chamber is covered.

Fig. 237: Covering the fire chamber with 2.4-in. (6 cm) thick fire-clay plates.

Fire Chamber Covering

and Chimney Connection

Tile oven and fireplace builders work according to a rhythm set by the materials used. (For example, quick-setting mortar sets considerably faster than firebrick mortar.) Thus the individual jobs were scheduled daily by the characteristics of the utilized materials. This also applied to covering the fire chamber, which began only after the parts of the fireplace already set (with mortar and plaster) could dry over the weekend (Fig. 236, 237). At the start of the following week the building of the fireplace could then be completed. This included the work of connecting the smoke pipe (11.8 in. or 30 cm diameter), which was equipped with a choke flap, with the upper part of the fire chamber (Fig. 238).

Fig. 238: The smoke pipe, set in quick-setting mortar, extends to shortly before the chimney opening.

Fig. 239: "Heat shielding" in the upper part of the fireplace; the chimney connection is seen at the rear.

Fig. 240: Covering the smoke pipe with fire-clay plates.

Since a very high temperature can be expected in the chimney connection area of this type of fireplace, it is important to protect the adjoining inner wall and the chimney connection with fire-clay plates (Fig. 239). Thus the smoke pipe (with choke flap) also had to be walled in with fire-clay plates (Fig. 240). The concrete ceiling above the connection was to be protected with an insulation plate to prevent the reinforcing iron in the concrete from getting hot, expanding and causing cracks (Fig. 241).

Shaping and Armament

Starting with the crude fireplace shape, as seen in Fig. 241, the builder began to form the final design. The still un-plastered part of the mantel was crudely covered with quick-setting mortar until it matched the shape of the model.

Fig. 241: The fireplace, as high as the room, has an insulating plate above the chimney connection.

Fig. 242: The builder uses potter mortar to form the raw shape of the fireplace. In the center is the rising wall of bricks for the final shaping.

shaping (center), can also be seen. It is interesting to see how the builder applies the potter mortar with the trowel (and a lot of concentration), thus preparing the final form of the fireplace.

After the base of the fireplace was plastered, the construction could dry out and set; then the last phase of the work was begun: setting armament fabric in quick-setting mortar and applying modeling plaster for the final shaping.

As described in previous chapters, the armament fabric had to be applied "wet-in-wet," a process in which the layer of quick-setting mortar had to be applied within a few minutes and armament fabric immediately pressed into it with a trowel. Then this armament layer was smoothed and shaped with a rubber trowel (Fig. 246).

In Fig. 242, this process is shown clearly. In this picture, the chimney connection (upper right) and the arched upward course of bricks, part of the final

Fig. 243: The last application of modeling plaster to the almost finished fireplace sculpture.

Fig. 244: The roughly plastered fireplace before the final modeling. In the opening is the 1:10 scale model.

Fig. 245: The armament fabric, reinforced with fiberglass.

Fig. 246: The builder smoothes and shapes the armament layer with a rubber trowel.

Fig. 247: The builder begins to apply and smooth the modeling plaster.

Fig. 248: Plastering the upper part of the fireplace sculpture, into which the chimney was also integrated.

Fig. 249: The same process on the lower part of the fireplace.

Fine Modeling

with Modeling Plaster

After all the uneven spots on the fireplace mantel were evened out with quick-setting mortar and smoothed with a rubber trowel, the fine modeling of the fireplace mantel with fine-grained plastering mortar began.

Since the modeling plaster sets within 30 to 45 minutes, it must be applied and smoothed very quickly so that time remains to smooth this last layer of plaster with a rubber trowel. The builder also used his hand to shape the last roundings (Fig. 250). Only after this modeling work was finished could the still-damp white plaster be smoothed with a rubber trowel (Fig. 252).

Fig. 250: With his left hand the builder models the outer rim of the fireplace opening.

Fig. 251: The fireplace mantel with
the hand-plastered opening.

Fig. 252: With the rubber trowel the builder ...

Fig. 252a: ...smoothes the modeling plaster.

After the fireplace mantel was covered with modeling plaster and the last uneven spots were smoothed, the builder began to plaster the base, the sitting surface of which was raised to the chimney to achieve the same shape as the model.

This shape also applied to the rim of the base, which was rounded by the builder's hands. It was a very gratifying experience to see how the fireplace sculpture came to look more and more like the model – to the last touch!

Fig. 253: The builder integrates the end of the base surface into the mantel.

Fig. 254: The edge of the base is rounded with a trowel.

Fig. 255: The completely plastered...

Fig. 255a: ...fireplace sculpture before the job was finished.

Fig. 256: The open fireplace in the living room. (Photo: Chiemton)

Fireplace 8:

The Masonry Fireplace and Round Oven

A Simple Shape Rediscovered

Whoever acquires a half-timbered country house that needs renovation will be interested in this fireplace/round oven, because it is a fireplace *and* a heating oven. The advantages are a crackling fire on the one hand and long-lasting heat storage on the other, which fills large rooms with radiated heat that is especially appreciated during the winter months.

Fig. 257: A free-standing bread oven in Lanzarote, Canary Islands.

Fig. 258: The masonry fireplace-round oven with smoke pipe (Fig. 258 and 260 to 289 by Felix Schleiermacher).

This fireplace/oven concept was presumably borrowed from the bread-baking ovens of rural regions, where it was built for decades, providing heat and practical uses. If the fire protection regulations are obeyed (your building inspector will know), this "fireplace" can be built very well by hand.

The prerequisites are a separate chimney flue (7.9 in. or 20 cm diameter), a fresh air intake (5.9 in. or 15 cm raw diameter), and a supporting cellar or floor that can carry over one ton of weight (850 kg to 900 kg).

Fireplace and Heat Reservoir

What makes this round fireplace/oven different from the fireplaces described before is not only its simple form and fireplace atmosphere, but also its ability to store heat.

This fireplace, built of firebricks, is also a heating oven into which two horizontal air ducts were built to gently reduce the speed of the smoke and store up to 80% of the fire-chamber heat in the fireplace mantel. The stored heat is given off into the room as radiating heat for 8 to 12 hours. Not hot air, just radiated heat!

Chimney and Fresh Air

Before the building materials were obtained from a builder's supply shop, the following details had to be cleared with the building inspector:

—Is a separate chimney or a chimney flue with a minimum diameter of 7.9 in. (20 cm) available?

—Is the length of the chimney sufficient (13 ft. or 4 m beyond the fireplace connection)?

—Is a sufficient fresh air supply available to equalize the low pressure during combustion? The raw diameter should be at least 6 in. (150 mm).

In addition, the strength of the floor must be tested, as the masonry oven weighs almost one ton (850 kg).

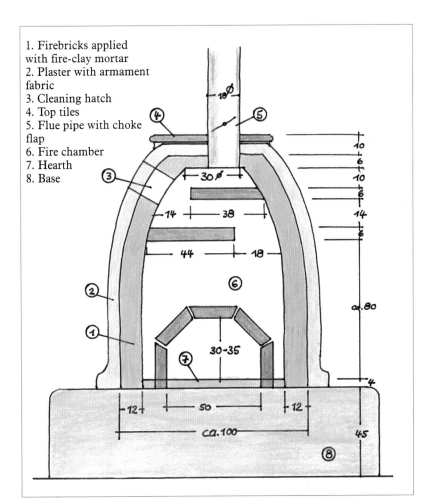

1. Firebricks applied with fire-clay mortar
2. Plaster with armament fabric
3. Cleaning hatch
4. Top tiles
5. Flue pipe with choke flap
6. Fire chamber
7. Hearth
8. Base

Fig. 259: Schematic drawing of the fireplace-oven (drawing from Bernd Grützmacher, *Kachelofenbaü*, Munich, Callwey, 1992).

Building the Foundation

In the first step of the work, the horizontal and vertical (17.7 in. or 45 cm) dimensions of the foundation were established after the circular surface of the oven (39.4 in. or 100 cm diameter) was marked on the concrete floor.

In this instance, the foundation was built directly on the concrete plate, whereby the "OFF" line was first to be established with lightweight bricks. This OFF surface was then the starting point for the actual base construction, which can be built with various materials. Should the base later be plastered, perforated bricks are suitable here, but if a visible masonry structure is wanted, then conventional bricks should be used.

The shape of the base is left to individual wishes, yet sitting surfaces should be planned, as they invite one to warm oneself on the fireplace wall on cold days!

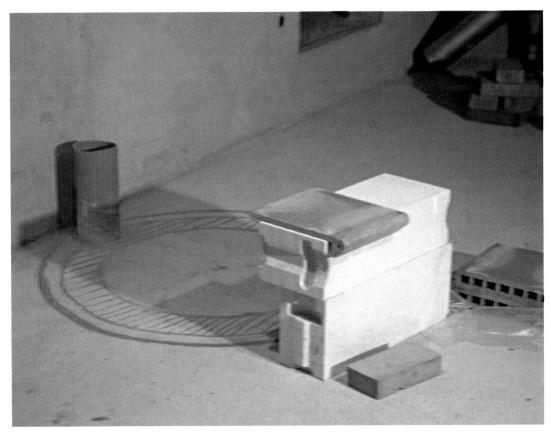

Fig. 260: The fresh air intake, circular markings and future seat level of the fireplace-oven.

Fig. 261: The foundation with fresh air opening but without outer brickwork.

Fig. 262: The bricked foundation shortly before the fire-chamber construction began.

Fig. 263: The baseplate of the fire chamber is finished around the level of the fireplace door and set in Haft mortar.

Fig. 264: The trapezoidal fireplace door as the starting point of the fireplace construction.

Normally, the base walls are set first, then the round foundation for the fireplace. The interstices can be filled last with stone rubble. Since the owner of this fireplace still had lightweight brick pieces left over, which could be cut easily, they were used for the inside of the base and then covered with brickwork for the sake of appearance.

Fire Chamber Floor

and Fireplace Opening

Though various materials for building the foundation are usable, only firebricks and plates should be used to build the fire chamber.

In Fig. 262 the foundation is finished and the round, cut baseplate of the fire chamber, which was laid in loose gravel to absorb future flexing, can be seen. The baseplate consists of four 2.4-in. (6 cm) thick fire-clay plates, which were cut precisely to fit. In the background are the firebricks for the fire chamber. This base construction indicates that the fireplace mantel was to be set not on the baseplate, but with a joint gap of 0.24 in. to 0.4 in. (6 mm to 10 mm), in order to prevent cracks in the fireplace mantel.

Before construction the fire chamber began, the fireplace door, the so-called "setting door," had to be on hand to be able to form the fireplace opening (Fig. 264). This double-walled door (with handle) should be made by a professional.

Fig. 265: Precise cutting of the firebricks for the fireplace opening.

Fig. 266: Beginning to build the fire chamber.

Because the door rests on the front baseplate of the fire chamber, the baseplate had to be finished in this area.

This step of the work must be done with special care, as the fireplace door, handmade by a metal smith, individually regulates the oxygen supply. The fireplace opening is determined by the dimensions of the fireplace door.

Since the firebricks for the frame of the fireplace opening must be cut to the sixteenth of an inch (note the vertical brick to

Fig. 267: The double-walled door of sheet steel between the vertical firebricks.

Fig. 268: The fire chamber while the fifth row of bricks is being set.

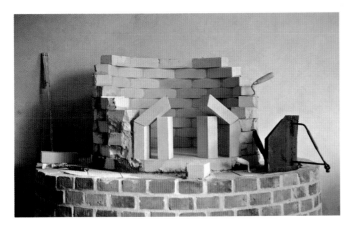

Fig. 269: The fireplace opening shortly before the top brick is cut, with the door at right.

Fig. 270: The frame construction of the fireplace opening.

Fig. 271: The fireplace opening with the door in place.

Fig. 272: The fire chamber up to the first air space.

the right of the door in Fig. 264), the builder "modeled" every piece of the fireplace opening with a cutter.

Fire Chamber and Flue Pipe

How the work begins is shown clearly in Fig. 266 and 267: In the foreground is the double-walled door with the vertical firebricks at the sides of the fireplace opening; adjoining them is the ring of the future fire chamber.

In these pictures, it can already be seen that only firebricks were used and cemented together.

While the fire chamber can be built without problems (a level will be helpful), the fireplace opening must be built with particular care. As can be seen in Fig. 269, the border bricks have to be cut very precisely and fitted dry so final corrections can be made. Only after these bricks had been cut correctly were they assembled with fireclay mortar.

As soon as the frame for the trapezoidal fireplace opening could bear a load, the fire-chamber construction was continued to a height of about 27.8 in. (75 cm). After the ninth row of bricks, the fireplace mantel begins to curve from there up (Fig. 272).

At this level, the construction of the first air space began. For it, a 2.4-in. (6 cm) thick fire-clay plate was cut to fit the round shape of the fireplace and set horizontally in fire-brick mortar. The opening between the plate edge and the fire chamber wall should measure at least 7.1 in. (18 cm) (see Fig. 259 and 273).

In our example, the smoke opening should be placed at the rear wall of the fire chamber. Two rows of bricks above it, the builder laid the second plate (Fig. 274), but this time with the opening to the front. At the same time, a cleaning hatch was built into the fire-chamber wall, big enough so that both plates can be cleaned by hand without problems.

Because of the inwardly curved shape of the fireplace, the covering of the fireplace/oven had to be set in mortar after two more rows of bricks and prepared for mounting the smoke pipe. This fire-clay plate (2.4 in. or 6 cm thick) was cut in a crude circular shape with an opening into which the

Fig. 273: The first air plate with the opening at the back (seen from above).

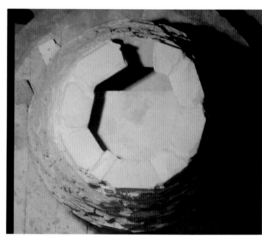

Fig. 274: The second air plate with the air opening and cleaning hatch to the front.

Fig. 275: The covering plate above the second air plate, with an opening for the smoke pipe.

Fig. 276: The top of the fire chamber before the double-walled duct for the flue pipe.

Fig. 277: The raw construction of the masonry fireplace-oven with the flue pipe to the chimney.

Fig. 278: The first test by fire!

double-walled mount for the smoke pipe (7 in. or 180 mm diameter) could be set.

Since this unusual construction was adapted from oven building, and because much water was needed for the mortar, it was important to test this raw structure with a hot fire (Fig. 278). For one thing, it would show how well the fireplace "drew," how fast flames and smoke were carried to the chimney; for another, the glowing fire would drive the dampness in the fire-chamber mantle to the outside, so that during this first burning a fog was created in the room. And that is good! The mass of masonry should "set," take its final form, before the plastering can begin. The cleaning hatch was temporarily covered for this first burning.

First Plastering

and Armament Fabric

At the beginning of the chapter, it was noted that this type of fireplace/round oven has existed for more than twenty years and still supplies heat to many country houses today.

Until a few years ago, it was customary to plaster the outside of it with firebrick mortar. In the still-damp mortar one then laid a tile-cord fabric ("Ziegelrabbitz"), which in turn was plastered. With this combination of materials, the powers of stretching were to be absorbed. One example shows this covering method (Fig. 279).

Fig. 279: The fireplace-oven is wrapped in tile-cord fabric and covered with firebrick mortar (still unapplied at the top).

Unfortunately, this tile-cord fabric is almost impossible to find in the trade. Instead, fiberglass-reinforced armament fabric was used, which could be applied faster and without problems, as shown in Fig. 280.

In any case, this job has to be carried out very quickly if quick-setting mortar is used instead of slowly-setting firebrick mortar. In our example, a fine-mesh armament fabric was used so that fast work was not possible. A wide-mesh fiberglass fabric, such as was described in Chapter 7 (Fig. 245), can also be recommended.

As always, the armament fabric should be laid on the large surface "wet-in-wet" and then smoothed with quick-setting mortar.

Fig. 280: The mantling of the fireplace-oven with fine-mesh armament fabric laid in quick-setting mortar.

Fig. 281: Laying the armament fabric on the upper mantel of the fireplace-oven.

Fig. 282: Modeling work around the fireplace opening.

Detailed Work Before

the Modeling Plaster

While the fabric-reinforced layer of plaster was still drying, the last details were completed. They included modeling the fireplace opening, covering the top of the fireplace/oven with handmade ceramic tiles, and installing the handmade ceramic sleeve (with decorative lid) for the cleaning hatch (4.7 in. or 12 cm diameter).

Fig. 283: The fireplace-oven plastered with quick-setting mortar, with the hand-finished covering tiles for the top shown in the foreground.

Fig. 284: Laying the tiles on top of the fireplace-oven.

Fig. 285: The handmade sleeve of the cleaning hatch, with a decorative lid.

Fig. 286: The first layer of modeling plaster is applied by hand...

Fig. 287: ...bonded with the armament fabric...

The Last Layer:

Modeling Plaster

This heat-resistant modeling plaster is normally applied quickly with a smoothing trowel, crudely smoothed and then finely structured with a rubber trowel. In this case, the homeowner wanted to apply it himself by hand in order to strengthen this last layer of plastering with the already used armament fabric, following the motto: Doubled holds better!

Since the owner did not like the crude surface formed by hand, the last uneven spots were corrected with a sponge until the desired shape was attained. Since then, the fireplace has been the focal point of evening sociability.

Fig. 288: ...and finally shaped crudely.

Appendix

Glossary

armament fabric – fiberglass-reinforced fabric set in quick-setting mortar to prevent cracks in fireplace walls.

baseplate – non-flammable plate to be installed for safety reasons. Suitable materials include granite, marble, glass, sheet steel, flagstones, and other non-flammable materials.

ceramic caulking strip – flexible buffer between the fireplace façade and masonry fireplace opening.

choke flap – closeable flap in the flue pipe with which the flow of smoke can be reduced.

corner braces – vertical or horizontal zinc-plated metal bars which protect corners and make plastering easier.

double-walled sleeve – flue-pipe attachment capable of bending, installed in the mantel of the fireplace.

fire chamber mortar – ceramic mortar for walls of fire chambers and flue pipes, to attach fire-clay bricks or tiles.

fire chamber walls – walls of fire bricks or tiles, with smoke collector and insulation to protect adjoining walls.

fire-clay bricks and plates – bricks and tiles made of clay with high resistance to temperature changes, great heat storage ability, and little heat expansion, basic material for fire chambers of open fireplaces.

fireplace – open masonry fire chamber with direct connection to a chimney, direct radiating warmth, low heat production, no heat-absorbing surfaces.

fireplace façade – exterior "frame" of a fireplace, made of cut or readymade parts, its various materials and shapes chosen by the homeowner.

fireplace mantel – fireplace components standing free of masonry, attached to the chimney and in many possible designs and shapes.

fireplace/oven – free-standing wood-burning oven for fast space heating, with visible fire behind adjustable glass door, "design object," simple to install, for the individual living milieu.

fireplace/oven I – prefabricated fireplace unit with raising panel and adjustable ceramic components, its heat-storage qualities create pleasant radiating heat but little convection heating.

fireplace/oven II – fireplace/oven with ceramic components, based on heavy fireplace/oven design, with high heat storage capacity, long-lasting radiation heating, and no convection heating.

floating concrete – coating removed from insulating surfaces, not suitable as a structural surface for fireplaces and stoves because it is not load-bearing.

flue channel – connection, either massive or of double-walled stainless steel ducts, between flue and chimney.

flue pipe – connection between the fire chamber and chimney that conducts smoke out.

fresh air duct – one is required for every furnace and tile oven to equalize the low air pressure created by burning and to supply oxygen for combustion.

hearth – the floor of the fire chamber, made of flexible fire-clay bricks or tiles.

heating fireplace – "open" prefabricated fireplace unit, often with a raising panel; high warm air quantity (convection heating), and little heat radiation if built to heat air.

hood – trapezoidal sheet-steel hood which leads smoke from fire chamber to flue pipe.

insulating plates – calcium silicate plates used to protect adjoining house walls from heat when building a fireplace or oven, conforming to fire safety regulations.

insulation – built-on walls, ceilings, and heat chambers are required to be covered with plates of insulation.

lightweight bricks – plate material suitable for the base and mantel of a prefabricated fireplace unit and for covering cold areas.

modeling plaster – fine-grained plaster mortar as the last plaster layer over the armament fabric, with which uneven spots on the fireplace mantel are smoothed.

perforated bricks – clay bricks in various shapes, pierced by holes, suitable for building fireplace and oven bases.

potter mortar – commercially produced fireproof plaster mortar for building tile ovens and fireplace chambers. High water content, slow setting time, long working time. To be moistened in advance.

quick-setting mortar – quickly setting wall mortar for ceramic and plaster materials in fireplace and oven building, also used as a shaping and modeling material. Not moistened in advance.

reinforced plates – fireproof fire-clay bricks or plates, covered with fiberglass armament, suitable for building radiation walls; they include curved plates for rounded fireplace designs. Applied only with quick-setting mortar.

smoke – the gas of burning that leaves the fire chamber.

stabilizing fabric – armament fabric superficially bonded with the outer ceramic layer (such as with modeling plaster) to prevent cracking.

ventilator flap – flap built into the fresh air pipe, by which the air intake can be closed.

The translator wishes to express his hearty thanks to the staff of Callwey GmbH for their help in translating the German technical terms into English.

Building and Assembling Tips*

—Open fireplaces can only be built when the ground surface and size of the space guarantee orderly operation (see DIN 18895, Part 1). Within the radiation area of the fireplace or fireplace unit there should be no structural components made of wood, concrete, or steel concrete.

—The open or "closed" fireplace may not be installed in spaces that are ventilated by ventilators (such as vacuum systems), unless there is a sufficient fresh air supply installed on the site to equalize the low air pressure in the space.

—It should be assured that the flue pipe between the fireplace and chimney is easy to clean. Besides, there should be no electric wires or gas pipes located in the area of the fireplace or fireplace unit (walls and ceilings).

—To equalize the low pressure and thus also the oxygen supply, a combustion air intake from outside should be ducted to the fireplace (minimum area 78.7 sq. in. or 200 sq. cm). Besides, the fresh air duct is to be equipped with a closing flap.

—Load-bearing building surfaces and floors of inflammable building materials must be protected by a layer of heat insulation at least 2.4 in. (6 cm)

thick before the work of building the fireplace begins.

—Adjoining walls (to the side and back) must be equipped with heat insulation. For wood-frame walls, a layer of masonry (such as lightweight brick) 3.9-in. (10 cm) thick must first be erected.

—Fireplace heating units are to be equipped with an outer mantel made of inflammable material so that an area of convection results, which gives off warmed air into the room through a hot-air grid.

—For the fireplace, a separate chimney is necessary, with a minimum length of 13 ft. (4 m) from the smoke-pipe connection.

—Extension joint: Between the fire chamber of an open fireplace and the "facade" of natural stone or metal, an extension joint is to be installed and enclosed with a heat-resistant caulking strip (such as a ceramic felt strip), in order to equalize flexing forces.

—Fire protection: In the radiation area of an open or "closed" fireplace, the floor must be covered to a distance of 31.5 in. (80 cm) with non-inflammable materials (tiles, marble, granite, steel, or glass).

*These tips are based on assembly instructions for fireplace installation by the firm of Sablux AG, Bachenbülach, Switzerland.

Photo Credits

All photos by the author, except the following: Chiemton: pages 1 and 2, plus Fig. 256; Peter Hackenberg: Fig. 51, 72; Feliz Schleiermacher: Fig. 258-289. Drawings from the author's archives unless otherwise noted.

Designs for Garden Paths. Heidi Howcroft. Garden walkways play a critical role in forming one's overall impression of a garden's entire arrangement and design. Using diagrams, layouts, and brilliant color photographs, this

invaluable guide describes the innumerable possibilities for garden walkways, terraces, steps, and cozy sitting areas. The book covers an array of surface options, including natural stone, modern concrete, and fantasy-filled mosaics, as well as wooden decks and other garden structures. Great for the professional or the weekend landscaper.

Size: 11" x 8 1/2"	149 color photos	127pp.
ISBN: 0-7643-0383-X	hard cover	$29.95

Retaining Walls: A Building Guide and Design Gallery. National Concrete Masonry Association, Tina Skinner. Whether it's a challenging hillside, an uneven backyard, or a shrubless plot in need of planters, this book will provide information to solve any landscaping dilemma while adding curb appeal and value to your property. The National Concrete Masonry Association presents the essential guide to constructing segmental re-

taining walls with detailed, easy-to-follow diagrams and charts for do-it-yourself homeowners and landscape contractors alike. From the fundamentals to the latest research and modern techniques in segmental retaining wall construction, this colorful and inspiring gallery of design suggestions accompanies the expertly written step-by-step guide, and offers a plethora of landscaping ideas. The exciting and attractive colors, textures, and styles of segmental retaining wall units available will inspire great new designs for all landscape styles.

Size: 8 1/2" x 11"	136 color photos,	128pp.
	22 b/w diagrams	
ISBN: 0-7643-1836-5	soft cover	$24.95

Patios, Driveways, and Plazas: The Pattern Language of Concrete Pavers. David R. Smith & the Interlocking Concrete Pavement Institute. Concrete pavers are one of the hottest pavements around homes, commercial buildings, and urban spaces. Designers know that the selection of pavement patterns and colors have a big influence on the character of these places. In this book, you'll learn the design vocabulary

of basic paving patterns and progress to more intricate variations. Each of the 300-plus color photos demonstrates how specific patterns, colors, and textures enhance every outdoor environment - including patios, walkways, drives, and grand urban plazas. Some of the best projects from across North America illustrate this book. Written for landscape architects, architects, contractors, and homeowners alike, this is the design handbook for concrete pavers. Besides presenting a wealth of ideas, the book will enrich and build your design vocabulary and pattern language using concrete pavers.

Size: 8 1/2" x 11"	327 photos	192pp.
ISBN: 0-7643-1561-7	soft cover	$29.95

Petite Patios & Intimate Garden Spaces. Gisela Keil, Nik Barlo Jr., and Christa Brand. Peek into hundreds of private backyards, where artists have crafted the most charming and intimate areas! Discover delightful dens hidden in the foliage or tucked on tiny terraces with beautiful vistas. Explore innovative ideas for designing and decorating private porches, patios, pagodas, and decks that provide the perfect space for outdoor living and

the intimacy of a small room. This book is packed with inspiration for spaces that provide escape, relaxation, meditation, and a small refuge for gathering. Share a glass of refreshment beneath generous branches of a nearby tree, laze about in a hammock, or stretch out on a bench and admire the tranquility of a pond, while relishing your secret hide-

away. This book is sure to motivate all who tire of life's everyday hassles to create their own intimate outdoor space.
Size: 8 1/2" x 11"   168 color photos   128 pp.
ISBN: 0-7643-2082-3   soft cover $19.95

All Decked Out...Redwood Decks: Ideas and Plans for Contemporary Outdoor Living. Tina Skinner. Redwood Decks: Ideas and Plans for Contemporary Outdoor Living is absolutely packed with more than 200 big, full-color photographs of fabulous decks from around the country, along with plans and building instructions for do-it-yourselfers. These great deck photos serve as a valuable resource for homeowners shopping

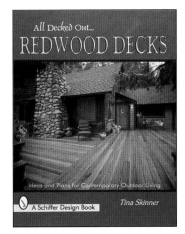

around for exciting deck ideas. Here you can find ideas for overcoming problem slopes, incorporating treasured trees, encircling spas, creating conversation pits, and enhancing gardens. It shows how simple additions, such as stylized railings or varied floor patterns, can evoke images of Japanese gardens or colonial elegance. For those who want to undertake their own construction project, there's a cut-out planner along with blueprints and lots of helpful hints to get you started. Redwood Decks is a complete start-up kit for anyone looking for ways to refocus their life in the great outdoors.
Size: 8 1/2" x 11"   212 color photos/31 illus. 160pp.
ISBN: 0-7643-0510-7   soft cover $29.95

Dream Kitchens: The Heart of the Home. John Olson & Cassidy Olson. The dream book of kitchens covers kitchens of every style and color. Visit hundreds of designer kitchens with professional photographers John and Cassidy Olson.

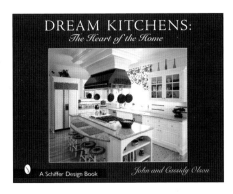

More than 300 inspired images of real-life kitchens provide you with the tools you need to begin transforming your kitchen into your dream. Each chapter highlights a particu-

lar design scheme and gives you many ideas on how to conceive of your own dream kitchen. Color schemes, design layout, and accessories are just some of the areas covered by this comprehensive picture book. Additionally, an entire chapter is devoted to pantries, one of the hottest kitchen inclusions for today's new and remodeled home projects.
Size: 11" x 8 1/2"   318 color photos   192pp.
ISBN: 0-7643-1757-1   hard cover $34.95

Architectural Ironwork. Dona Z. Meilach. This new book showcases a vast array of ironwork commissioned for new commercial and residential building projects. Traditional styles in modern settings and designs that reach for new visual impact help to redefine ironwork's status in our current society. There are over 375 spectacular examples from more than 100 of today's top blacksmiths, supplemented

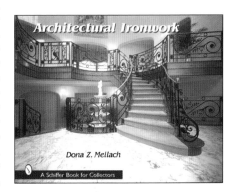

with historical works from 15 countries, some derived from old French and English ironwork. These include doors and hardware, staircases and railings, and gates and fences. This book will inspire architects, builders, homeowners, and artist-blacksmiths with the wealth of beautiful ideas it contains.

Size: 11" x 8 1/2"   233 color &   256pp.
                         53 b/w photos
ISBN: 0-7643-1324-X   hard cover $49.95

Ceramic Art Tile for the Home. DeBorah Goletz. Art tile is a truly exciting option for both interior and exterior decoration. There is a vast array of tile available on the market today, ranging in design from traditional to modern, and conservative to outrageous—the possibilities are overwhelming! This book is a wonderful introduction to art tile, loaded with ideas and resources that will charm and inspire. Hun-

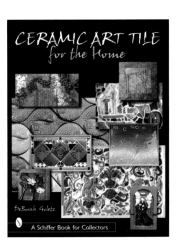

dreds of breathtaking photographs of installations in and out of the home show the work of today's leading contemporary tile artists. Insightful text guides readers to an informed appreciation of this timeless art and its marvelous suitability for all areas of the home. Chapters include a history of tile making in America, how art tile is made, visiting a tile showroom, designing with art tile, trends in art tile, what to expect during installation, and ceramic art in public spaces. A large resource index and a directory of artists is included.

Size: 8 1/2" x 11"   265 color photos   160pp.
ISBN: 0-7643-1297-9   soft cover $29.95

Bright Ideas: Sunrooms & Conservatories. Tina Skinner. This rich compendium of color photos shows interior and exterior shots of sunrooms, conservatories, greenhouses, and great glass walls will help homeowners, architects, and remodelers choose the perfect addition. These images will help you select the right style for your architecture, as well as your lifestyle. There are plenty of ideas for furnishing your indoor extension into the

great outdoors, from formal dining areas to comfy family gathering spots. There are tub and pool rooms, patio rooms and indoor gardens, even kitchens and fanciful Florida rooms. If more than two people will use a new home addition, it's important that both agree on styles and furnishings. Here's a great, one-stop planning resource to help mesh your individual tastes, with resources listed to help you make your vision a reality.

Size: 8 1/2" x 11"   189 photos   160pp.
ISBN: 0-7643-1418-1   soft cover $29.95

Great Kitchen Designs: A Visual Feast of Ideas and Resources. Tina Skinner. Here is a collection of 370 gorgeous color photos to pour over and ponder: images to inspire dreams. Full-color pictures of hundreds of beautiful kitchens will help you sort out the details and create your own unique cooking/dining/entertaining environment. All the elements of beautiful kitchens-flooring, cabinetry, windows, walls, lighting, appliances, surrounds, backsplashes and more —are pictured and discussed. Individual chapters will help you find the right look, exploring current trends from exotic to country, formal to feminine, antique to modern. Imaginative solutions for showing off collections are explored, as well as ways to open up the kitchen to wonderful outside views.

There are lots of ideas for creating gathering places for family and guests alike into the hearth of the home. A special chapter on the small kitchen illustrates solutions for homes with limited space, and a resource guide at the back of the book will point you toward award-winning designers and top-notch manufacturers. This is an invaluable resource for anyone planning to remodel an old kitchen or build a new one and a great reference book and sales tool for any kitchen design professional.

Size: 8 1/2" x 11"   370 color photos   176pp.
ISBN: 0-7643-1211-1   soft cover $29.95

Designs for Restaurants & Bars: Inspiration from Hundreds of International Hotels. Tina Skinner. Here is a sumptuous banquet of the hospitality world's finest offerings in places to eat and drink. Tour more than 200 designer and boutique hotels from around the world, along with classics such as The Ritz in London, The Oriental Bangkok, the New York Palace Hotel, and the Hôtel Plaza Athénée in Paris. Top hotel and restaurant design firms from around the world are included, with industry leaders such as David Rockwell, Ian Schrager, Robert DiLeonardo, and Adam

Tihany. Plus, there is work by design world icons Karl Lagerfeld, Pierre Court, Patrick Jouin, and Philippe Starck. The visual banquet includes classic European designs dripping in decorative molding and custom paneling, gold leaf and crystal chandeliers. There are starkly modern designs, fashionable Asian Fusion and eclectic settings, and tropical paradises, as well as playful and erotic designs. A resource guide provides contact information for design and architectural firms, as well as the beautiful establishments shown. This is an inspiring book for anyone planning or designing a place of hospitality and consumption.

Size: 8 1/2" x 11"   256 color photos   176pp.
ISBN: 0-7643-1752-0   soft cover $39.95